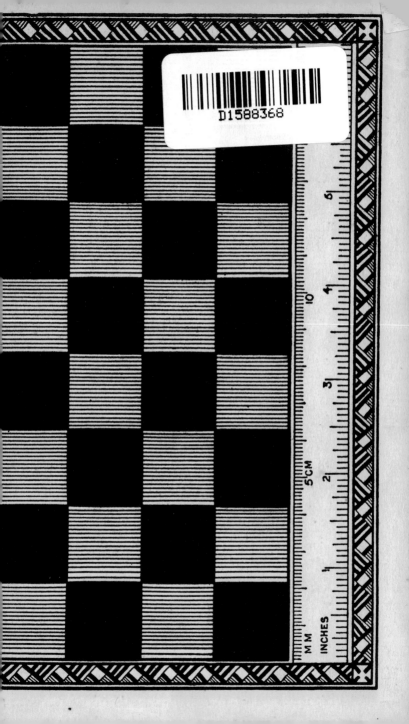

"All that was left of them"
After the Fray

" COOPER EXHIBITS."

Q.h.B. Quick. Gl Alleny Surgeon   D. Wainwright   Dunning
    Field d Staff.   Assist then Man   Vet Surg.

THE WEEK-END BOOK

THE
WEEK-END
BOOK

1925
THE NONESUCH PRESS
16 GREAT JAMES STREET
LONDON

FIRST IMPRESSION . . JUNE, 1924

SECOND IMPRESSION . . JUNE, 1924

THIRD IMPRESSION . . JULY, 1924

FOURTH IMPRESSION . . JULY, 1924

FIFTH IMPRESSION . SEPTEMBER, 1924

SIXTH IMPRESSION . DECEMBER, 1924

SEVENTH IMPRESSION . DECEMBER, 1924

EIGHTH IMPRESSION (ENLARGED
AND REVISED) . . . MARCH, 1925

NINTH IMPRESSION (INDIA
PAPER) . . . . APRIL, 1925

TENTH IMPRESSION . . JUNE, 1925

WEEK-END

The train ! The twelve o'clock for paradise.
Hurry, or it will try to creep away.
Out in the country everyone is wise :
We can be only wise on Saturday.
There you are waiting, little friendly house :
Those are your chimney-stacks with you between,
Surrounded by old trees and strolling cows,
Staring through all your windows at the green.
Your homely floor is creaking for our tread ;
The smiling tea-pot with contented spout
Thinks of the boiling water, and the bread
Longs for the butter.   All their hands are out
To greet us, and the gentle blankets seem
Purring and crooning : " Lie in us, and dream."

Harold Monro.

THE CONTENTS

THE WEEK-END BOOK explains itself. A preface can but italicize the anthological principles of the editors. The first of these is the axiom that there are no good anthologies, always excepting the one which every man would like to make himself—with a newly revised, abridged and amplified edition every five years or so. We have accordingly attempted to meet every man half-way and to compile a book of clues to good life and reading for week-end pairs and parties, which each in his fashion may follow up. We hope to have as many collaborators as readers ; and to make it easy for them to amplify our design we have included a section of blank pages of writing paper. As for abridgment, we have saved them trouble by printing the titles, first lines and authors only, of those great poems which their pastors and masters in infancy and their poetic enthusiasms in adolescence have already made sufficiently, if not excessively, familiar. These may be transcribed on the blank pages at the end of the book, or recited or banished from memory, according to individual taste and ability.

Subject to our first anthological principle, we trust that this pocketful of poetry will, in the main, satisfy the Georgian version of the " Open Road " public. For, after all, there is a consensus of opinion between generations, called taste : not to speak of fashion, that even closer coincidence of appreciation within generations. As it is designed to supplement and balance the Oxford Book of English Verse (carried in the opposite pocket) we have sought out the less familiar of the great poems, poets and periods. The anthology pieces of any author have been avoided wherever there is a worthy alternative.

ix

PREFACE

Shakespeare and the Romantics are charily presented, the Augustans not at all. The poetry of the seventeenth century, which school text-books most inadequately present, and that of the twentieth century, which older anthologies perforce ignore, is most amply represented.

The section of Great *Poems* is arranged in chronological order and takes no account of subjects. Love poetry and Nature poetry must take so large a place in any general collection of great poems that lovers and land-lovers need no separate provision. But some pleasant and some poignant verse sprung from the mood of hate has been grouped together for the specific enjoyment of that almost as widely felt emotion. The State poems need no comment. They provide an outlet for yet another mood, not uncommon in hours of sociable relaxation. " The Zoo " should appeal to the collector's temperament. Those who take up the pleasant hobby of zoological literature will find material among the poets for building a handsome collection around this nuclear section.

The *Songs* are ransacked from all ages, countries and moods, the only " unity " observed by the compiler being that of fitness for purpose—the sociable week-ender's purpose. They are some of the best available tunes for unaccompanied chorus singing, only occasionally and effectively to be varied by a solo and chorus rendering. Moreover, they are all folk songs, in the spirit of the word —and the letter too if, as we may fairly contend, the term covers such newer equivalents as " shanties," " spirituals " and the spontaneous effusions of the British Expeditionary Force. Such a collection, we believe, is at present unique.

The *three prose sections* contain the most useful hints which we have been able to gather on the food, drink, diversions and damages of week-enders. They postulate the cookless cottage, the camp fire, or the restricted resources of a country pub. The suggestions contained in the play section also involve no more than that two or three be gathered together with such readily accessible or improvised implements as a stick and ball or a pencil and paper. The medical prescriptions are contributed by a practising physician ; they contain only such ingredients and doses as may be supplied by a chemist without recourse to a personal prescription.

> VERA MENDEL
> FRANCIS MEYNELL
> > *General Editors.*
> JOHN GOSS
> > *Music Editor.*

PREFACE TO THE SECOND EDITION

ON publishing this book last year we had occasion to thank some of our friends for providing sundry ideas, facts, and paragraphs which were incorporated in its original form. Since then, as we had hoped, many of our readers have become co-editors in amplifying its various sections. From all parts of the world they have communicated to us the contents of their manuscript pages. We gratefully acknowledge their suggestions and have accordingly added a number of poems and songs to this edition. We have also included a new section, containing epigrams, epitaphs, limericks and the like. " *On Food and Drink* " has been revised and enlarged by an expert in the

theory and practice of cookery, so that ambitious week-
end hostesses, as well as more elementary practitioners,
may profitably consult it. At the end of the book, we
print the latest variant of that time-honoured favourite
the "confessions book," in which self-portraits stand
sociably corrected. We are glad of this opportunity once
more to thank all those co-operators who have left their
mark upon this book.

V . M .

F . M .

J . G .

GREAT POEMS

B

" A book of verses underneath the bough."
Omar Khayyam.

O WESTERN WIND

O WESTERN wind, when wilt thou blow,
 That the small rain down can rain?
Christ, that my love were in my arms
 And I in my bed again!

Anonymous.

HEY NONNY NO!

HEY nonny no!
Men are fools that wish to die!
Is't not fine to dance and sing
When the bells of death do ring?
Is't not fine to swim in wine,
And turn upon the toe,
And sing hey nonny no!
When the winds blow and the seas flow?
Hey nonny no!

Anonymous.

JOLY JOLY WAT

THE shepherd upon a hill he sat;
He had on him his tabard and his hat,
His tarbox, his pipe, and his flagat;
His name was called Joly Joly Wat,
For he was a good herdes boy
   Ut hoy!
For in his pipe he made so much joy.

The shepherd upon a hill was laid;
His dog to his girdle was tied;
He had not slept but a little braid,
But " *Gloria in excelsis* " was to him said.
   Ut hoy!
For in his pipe he made so much joy.

3

The shepherd on a hill he stood ;
Round about him his sheep they yode ;
He put his hand under his hood,
He saw a star as red as blood.
      Ut hoy !
  For in his pipe he made so much joy.

The shepherd said anon right,
" I will go see yon farly sight,
Whereas the angel singeth on height,
And the star that shineth so bright."
      Ut hoy !
  For in his pipe he made so much joy.

" Now farewell, Moll, and also Will !
For my love go ye all still
Unto I come again you till,
And evermore, Will, ring well thy bell."
      Ut hoy !
  For in his pipe he made so much joy.

" Now must I go there Christ was born ;
Farewell !   I come again to morn.
Dog, keep well my sheep from the corn,
And warn well ' Warroke ' when I blow my horn ! "
      Ut hoy !
  For in his pipe he made so much joy.

When Wat to Bethlehem come was,
He sweat, he had gone faster than a pace ;
He found Jesu in a simple place,
Between an ox and an ass.
      Ut hoy !
  For in his pipe he made so much joy.

" Jesu, I offer to thee here my pipe,
My skirt, my tarbox, and my scrip ;
Home to my fellows now will I skip,
And also look unto my sheep."
      Ut hoy !
  For in his pipe he made so much joy.

4

" Now farewell, mine own herdsman Wat ! "
" Yea, for God, lady, even so I hight ;
Lull well Jesu in thy lap,
And farewell, Joseph, with thy round cape ! "
Ut hoy !
For in his pipe he made so much joy.

" Now may I well both hope and sing,
For I have been at Christ's bearing ;
Home to my fellows now will I fling,
Christ of heaven to his bliss us bring ! "
Ut hoy!
For in his pipe he made so much joy.

Anonymous.

I SING OF A MAIDEN

I SING of a maiden
   That is makeless.
King of all kinges
   To her son she chose.

He came all so stille
   There his mother was
As dew in Aprille
   That falleth on grass.

He came all so stille
   To his mother's bower,
As dew in Aprille
   That falleth on the flower.

He came all so stille
   There his mother lay,
As dew in Aprille
   That falleth on the spray.

Mother and maiden
   Was never none but she ;
Well may such a lady
   Godes mother be.

Anonymous.

5

JOLLY GOOD ALE AND OLD

I CANNOT eat but little meat,
    My stomach is not good;
But sure I think that I can drink
    With him that wears a hood.
Though I go bare, take ye no care,
    I nothing am a-cold;
I stuff my skin so full within
    Of jolly good ale and old.
        Back and side go bare, go bare;
        Both foot and hand go cold;
        But, belly, God send thee good ale enough,
        Whether it be new or old.

I love no roast but a nut-brown toast,
    And a crab laid in the fire;
A little bread shall do me stead;
    Much bread I not desire.
No frost nor snow, no wind, I trow,
    Can hurt me if I wold;
I am so wrapped and thoroughly lapped
    Of jolly good ale and old.
        Back and side go bare, go bare, etc.

And Tib, my wife, that as her life
    Loveth well good ale to seek,
Full oft drinks she till ye may see
    The tears run down her cheek:
Then doth she trowl to me the bowl
    Even as a maltworm should,
And saith, " Sweetheart, I took my part
    Of this jolly good ale and old."
        Back and side go bare, go bare, etc.

Now let them drink till they nod and wink,
    Even as good fellows should do;
They shall not miss to have the bliss
    Good ale doth bring men to;
And all poor souls that have scoured bowls
    Or have them lustily trolled,
God save the lives of them and their wives,
    Whether they be young or old.

Back and side go bare, go bare;
Both foot and hand go cold;
But, belly, God send thee good ale enough,
Whether it be new or old.
                    John Still (Bishop of Bath and Wells).

WALY, WALY

O WALY, waly, up the bank,
  And waly, waly, doun the brae,
And waly, waly, yon burn-side,
  Where I and my Love wont to gae!
I lean'd my back unto an aik,
  I thocht it was a trustie tree;
But first it bow'd and syne it brak—
  Sae my true love did lichtlie me.

O waly, waly, gin love be bonnie
  A little time while it is new!
But when 'tis auld it waxeth cauld,
  And fades awa' like morning dew.
O wherefore should I busk my heid,
  Or wherefore should I kame my hair?
For my true Love has me forsook,
  And says he'll never lo'e me mair.

Now Arthur's Seat sall be my bed,
  The sheets sall ne'er be 'filed by me;
Saint Anton's well sall be my drink,
  Since my true Love has forsaken me;
Marti'mas wind, when wilt thou blaw,
  And shake the green leaves aff the tree?
O gentle Death, when wilt thou come?
  For of my life I am wearie.

'Tis not the frost, that freezes fell,
  Nor blawing snaw's inclemencie,
'Tis not sic cauld that makes me cry;
  But my Love's heart grown cauld to me.
When we cam in by Glasgow toun,
  We were a comely sicht to see;
My Love was clad in the black velvet,
  And I mysel in cramasie.

7

But had I wist, before I kist,
  That love had been sae ill to win,
I had lock'd my heart in a case o' gowd,
  And pinn'd it wi' a siller pin.
And O ! if my young babe were born,
  And set upon the nurse's knee ;
And I mysel were dead and gane,
  And the green grass growing over me !

Anonymous.

HELEN OF KIRCONNELL

I WISH I were where Helen lies,
Night and day on me she cries ;
O that I were where Helen lies,
  On fair Kirconnell lea !

Curst be the heart that thought the thought,
And curst the hand that fired the shot,
When in my arms burd Helen dropt,
  And died to succour me !

O think na ye my heart was sair,
When my Love dropp'd and spak nae mair !
There did she swoon wi' meikle care,
  On fair Kirconnell lea.

As I went down the water side,
None but my foe to be my guide,
None but my foe to be my guide,
  On fair Kirconnell lea ;

I lighted down my sword to draw,
I hacked him in pieces sma',
I hacked him in pieces sma',
  For her sake that died for me.

O Helen fair, beyond compare !
I'll mak a garland o' thy hair,
Shall bind my heart for evermair,
  Until the day I die !

8

O that I were where Helen lies !
Night and day on me she cries ;
Out of my bed she bids me rise,
    Says, " Haste, and come to me ! "

O Helen fair !   O Helen chaste !
If I were with thee, I'd be blest,
Where thou lies low and taks thy rest,
    On fair Kirconnell lea.

I wish my grave were growing green,
A winding-sheet drawn owre my e'en,
And I in Helen's arms lying,
    On fair Kirconnell lea.

I wish I were where Helen lies !
Night and day on me she cries ;
And I am weary of the skies,
    For her sake that died for me.

Anonymous.

THE BONNY EARL OF MURRAY

Y E Highlands and ye Lawlands,
    O where hae ye been ?
They hae slain the Earl of Murray,
    And hae laid him on the green.

Now wae be to thee, Huntley !
    And whairfore did ye sae !
I bade you bring him wi' you,
    But forbade you him to slay.

He was a braw gallant,
    And he rid at the ring ;
And the bonny Earl of Murray,
    O he might hae been a king !

He was a braw gallant,
    And he play'd at the ba' ;
And the bonny Earl of Murray
    Was the flower amang them a' !

He was a braw gallant,
  And he play'd at the gluve;
And the bonny Earl of Murray,
  O he was the Queen's luve!

O lang will his Lady
  Look owre the Castle Downe,
Ere she see the Earl of Murray
  Come sounding through the town!

Anonymous.

THE QUEEN'S MARIE

MARIE HAMILTON'S to the kirk gane,
  Wi' ribbons in her hair;
The King thought mair o' Marie Hamilton
  Than ony that were there.

Marie Hamilton's to the kirk gane
  Wi' ribbons on her breast;
The King thought mair o' Marie Hamilton
  Than he listen'd to the priest.

Marie Hamilton's to the kirk gane,
  Wi' gloves upon her hands;
The King thought mair o' Marie Hamilton
  Than the Queen and a' her lands.

She hadna been about the King's court
  A month but barely one,
Till she was beloved by a' King's court
  And the King the only man.

She hadna been about the King's court
  A month, but barely three,
Till frae the King's court Marie Hamilton,
  Marie Hamilton durstna be.

The King is to the Abbey gane,
  To pu' the Abbey tree,
To scale the babe frae Marie's heart;
  But the thing it wadna be.

O she has row'd it in her apron,
   And set it on the sea—
" Gae sink ye or swim ye, bonny babe,
   Ye'se get nae mair o' me."

Word is to the kitchen gane,
   And word is to the ha',
And word is to the noble room
   Amang the ladies a',
That Marie Hamilton's brought to bed,
   And the bonny babe's miss'd and awa'.

Scarcely had she lain down again,
   And scarcely fa'en asleep,
When up and started our gude Queen
   Just at her bed-feet;
Saying—" Marie Hamilton, where's your babe ?
   For I am sure I heard it greet."

" O no, O no, my noble Queen !
   Think no sic thing to be;
'Twas but a stitch into my side,
   And sair it troubles me !"

" Get up, get up, Marie Hamilton :
   Get up and follow me ;
For I am going to Edinburgh town,
   A rich wedding for to see."

O slowly, slowly rase she up,
   And slowly put she on ;
And slowly rade she out the way
   Wi' mony a weary groan.

The Queen was clad in scarlet,
   Her merry maids all in green ;
And every town that they cam to,
   They took Marie for the Queen.

" Ride hooly, hooly, gentlemen,
   Ride hooly now wi' me !
For never, I am sure, a wearier burd
   Rade in your companie."—

But little wist Marie Hamilton,
  When she rade on the brown,
That she was gaen to Edinburgh town
  And a' to be put down.

" Why weep ye so, ye burgess wives,
  Why look ye so on me ?
O I am going to Edinburgh town.
  A rich wedding to see."

When she gaed up the tolbooth stairs,
  The corks frae her heels did flee ;
And lang or e'er she cam down again,
  She was condemn'd to die.

When she cam to the Netherbow port,
  She laugh'd loud laughters three ;
But when she came to the gallows foot
  The tears blinded her e'e.

" Yestreen the Queen had four Maries.
  The night she'll hae but three ;
There was Marie Seaton, and Marie Beaton,
  And Marie Carmichael, and me.

" O often have I dress'd my Queen
  And put gowd upon her hair ;
But now I've gotten for my reward
  The gallows to be my share.

" Often have I dress'd my Queen
  And often made her bed ;
But now I've gotten for my reward
  The gallows tree to tread.

" I charge ye all, ye mariners,
  When ye sail owre the faem,
Let neither my father nor mother get wit
  But that I'm coming hame.

" I charge ye all, ye mariners,
  That sail upon the sea,
That neither my father nor mother get wit
  The dog's death I'm to die.

" For if my father and mother got wit,
  And my bold brethren three,
O mickle wad be the gude red blude
  This day wad be spilt for me !

" O little did my mother ken,
  The day she cradled me
The lands I was to travel in
  Or the death I was to die ! "

Anonymous.

CLERK SAUNDERS

CLERK SAUNDERS and may Margaret
  Walk'd owre yon garden green ;
And deep and heavy was the love
  That fell thir twa between.

" A bed, a bed," Clerk Saunders said,
  " A bed for you and me ! "
" Fye na, fye na," said may Margaret,
  " Till anes we married be ! "

" Then I'll take the sword frae my scabbard
  And slowly lift the pin ;
And you may swear, and save your aith,
  Ye ne'er let Clerk Saunders in.

" Take you a napkin in your hand,
  And tie up baith your bonnie e'en,
And you may swear, and save your aith,
  Ye saw me na since late yestreen."

It was about the midnight hour,
  When they asleep were laid,
When in and came her seven brothers,
  Wi' torches burning red ;

When in and came her seven brothers,
  Wi' torches burning bright :
They said, " We hae but one sister,
  And behold her lying with a knight ! "

Then out and spake the first o' them,
   " I bear the sword shall gar him die."
And out and spake the second o' them,
   " His father has nae mair but he."

And out and spake the third o' them,
   " I wot that they are lovers dear."
And out and spake the fourth o' them,
   " They hae been in love this mony a year."

Then out and spake the fifth o' them,
   " It were great sin true love to twain."
And out and spake the sixth o' them,
   " It were shame to slay a sleeping man."

Then up and gat the seventh o' them.
   And never a word spake he ;
But he has striped his bright brand
   Out through Clerk Saunders' fair body.

Clerk Saunders he started, and Margaret she turn'd
   Into his arms as asleep she lay ;
And sad and silent was the night
   That was atween thir twae.

And they lay still and sleepit sound
   Until the day began to daw' ;
And kindly she to him did say,
   " It is time, true love, you were awa'."

But he lay still, and sleepit sound,
   Albeit the sun began to sheen ;
She look'd atween her and the wa',
   And dull and drowsie were his e'en.

Then in and came her father dear ;
   Said, " Let a' your mourning be ;
I'll carry the dead corse to the clay,
   And I'll come back and comfort thee."

" Comfort weel your seven sons,
   For comforted I will never be :
I ween 'twas neither knave nor loon
   Was in the bower last night wi' me."

The clinking bell gaed through the town,
   To carry the dead corse to the clay;
And Clerk Saunders stood at may Margaret's
   window,
   I wot, an hour before the day.

" Are ye sleeping, Margaret ? " he says,
   " Or are ye waking presently ?
Give me my faith and troth again,
   I wot, true love, I gied to thee."

" Your faith and troth ye sall never get,
   Nor our true love sall never twin,
Until ye come within my bower,
   And kiss me cheik and chin."

" My mouth it is full cold, Marg'ret;
   It has the smell, now, of the ground;
And if I kiss thy comely mouth,
   Thy days of life will not be lang.

" O cocks are crowing a merry midnight;
   I wot the wild fowls are boding day;
Give me my faith and troth again,
   And let me fare me on my way."

" Thy faith and troth thou sallna get,
   And our true love sall never twin,
Until ye tell what comes o' women,
   I wot, who die in strong traivelling ? "

" Their beds are made in the heavens high,
   Down at the foot of our good Lord's knee,
Weel set about wi' gillyflowers;
   I wot, sweet company for to see.

" O cocks are crowing a merry midnight;
   I wot the wild fowls are boding day;
The psalms of heaven will soon be sung,
   And I, ere now, will be miss'd away."

Then she has taken a crystal wand,
   And she has stroken her troth thereon;
She has given it him out at the shot-window,
   Wi' mony a sad sigh and heavy groan.

" I thank ye, Marg'ret ; I thank ye, Marg'ret ;
  And ay I thank ye heartily ;
Gin ever the dead come for the quick,
  Be sure, Marg'ret, I'll come for thee."

It's hosen and shoon, and gown alone,
  She climb'd the wall, and follow'd him,
Until she came to the green forest,
  And there she lost the sight o' him.

" Is there ony room at your head, Saunders ?
  Is there ony room at your feet ?
Or ony room at your side, Saunders,
  Where fain, fain, I wad sleep ? "

" There's nae room at my head, Marg'ret,
  There's nay room at my feet ;
My bed it is fu' lowly now,
  Amang the hungry worms I sleep.

" Cauld mould is my covering now,
  But and my winding-sheet ;
The dew it falls nae sooner down
  Than my resting-place is weet.

" But plait a wand o' bonny birk,
  And lay it on my breast ;
And shed a tear upon my grave,
  And wish my saul gude rest."

Then up and crew the red, red cock,
  And up and crew the gray ;
" 'Tis time, 'tis time, my dear Marg'ret,
  That you were going away.

" And fair Marg'ret, and rare Marg'ret,
  And Marg'ret o' veritie,
Gin e'er ye love another man,
  Ne'er love him as ye did me."

Anonymous.

THE LAMENT OF DAVID OVER SAUL AND JONATHAN

T H E beauty of Israel is slain upon thy high places : how are the mighty fallen !

Tell it not in Gath, publish it not in the streets of Askelon ; lest the daughters of the Philistines rejoice, lest the daughters of the uncircumcised triumph.

Ye mountains of Gilboa, let there be no dew, neither let there be rain, upon you, nor fields of offerings : for there the shield of the mighty is vilely cast away, the shield of Saul, as though he had not been anointed with oil.

From the blood of the slain, from the fat of the mighty, the bow of Jonathan turned not back, and the sword of Saul returned not empty.

Saul and Jonathan were lovely and pleasant in their lives, and in their death they were not divided : they were swifter than eagles, they were stronger than lions.

Ye daughters of Israel, weep over Saul, who clothed you in scarlet, with other delights, who put on ornaments of gold upon your apparel.

How are the migthy fallen in the midst of the battle ! O Jonathan, thou wast slain in thine high places.

I am distressed for thee, my brother Jonathan : very pleasant hast thou been unto me : thy love to me was wonderful, passing the love of women.

How are the mighty fallen, and the weapons of war perished !

Authorised Version.

PSALM 137

B Y the waters of Babylon we sat down and wept : when we remembered thee, O Sion.

As for our harps, we hanged them up : upon the trees that are therein.

For they that led us away captive required of us then a song, and melody, in our heaviness : Sing us one of the songs of Sion.

How shall we sing the Lord's song : in a strange land ?

If I forget thee, O Jerusalem : let my right hand forget her cunning.

If I do not remember thee, let my tongue cleave to the roof of my mouth : yea, if I prefer not Jerusalem in my mirth.

Remember the children of Edom, O Lord, in the day of Jerusalem : how they said, Down with it, down with it, even to the ground.

O daughter of Babylon, wasted with misery : yea, happy shall he be that rewardeth thee, as thou hast served us.

Blessed shall he be that taketh thy children : and throweth them against the stones.

The " Great Bible."

THE SONG OF SONGS, WHICH IS SOLOMON'S

I

LET him kiss me with the kisses of his mouth : for thy love is better than wine.

Because of the savour of thy good ointments thy name is as ointment poured forth, therefore do the virgins love thee.

Draw me, we will run after thee : the king hath brought me into his chambers : we will be glad and rejoice in thee, we will remember thy love more than wine : the upright love thee.

I am black, but comely, O ye daughters of Jerusalem, as the tents of Kedar, as the curtains of Solomon.

Look not upon me, because I am black, because the sun hath looked upon me : my mother's children were angry with me ; they made me the keeper of the vineyards ; but mine own vineyard have I not kept.

Tell me, O thou whom my soul loveth, where thou feedest, where thou makest thy flock to rest at noon : for why should I be as one that turneth aside by the flocks of thy companions ?

If thou know not, O thou fairest among women, go thy way forth by the footsteps of the flock, and feed thy kids beside the shepherds' tents.

I have compared thee, O my love, to a company of horses in Pharaoh's chariots.

Thy cheeks are comely with rows of jewels, thy neck with chains of gold.

We will make thee borders of gold with studs of silver.

While the king sitteth at his table, my spikenard sendeth forth the smell thereof.

A bundle of myrrh is my wellbeloved unto me; he shall lie all night betwixt my breasts.

My beloved is unto me as a cluster of camphire in the vineyards of En-gedi.

Behold, thou art fair, my love; behold, thou art fair; thou hast doves' eyes.

Behold, thou art fair, my beloved, yea, pleasant: also our bed is green.

The beams of our house are cedar, and our rafters of fir.

II

I AM the rose of Sharon, and the lily of the valleys.

As the lily among thorns, so is my love among the daughters.

As the apple tree among the trees of the wood, so is my beloved among the sons. I sat down under his shadow with great delight, and his fruit was sweet to my taste.

He brought me to the banqueting house, and his banner over me was love.

Stay me with flagons, comfort me with apples: for I am sick of love.

His left hand is under my head, and his right hand doth embrace me.

I charge you, O ye daughters of Jerusalem, by the roes, and by the hinds of the field, that ye stir not up, nor awake my love, till he please.

The voice of my beloved! behold, he cometh leaping upon the mountains, skipping upon the hills.

My beloved is like a roe or a young hart: behold he, standeth behind our wall, he looketh forth at the windows, shewing himself through the lattice.

My beloved spake, and said unto me, Rise up, my love, my fair one, and come away.

For, lo, the winter is past, the rain is over and gone;

The flowers appear on the earth; the time of the singing of birds is come, and the voice of the turtle is heard in our land;

The fig tree putteth forth her green figs, and the vines with the tender grape give a good smell. Arise, my love, my fair one, and come away.

O my dove, that art in the clefts of the rock, in the secret places of the stairs, let me see thy countenance, let me hear thy voice; for sweet is thy voice, and thy countenance is comely.

Take us the foxes, the little foxes, that spoil the vines: for our vines have tender grapes.

My beloved is mine, and I am his: he feedeth among the lilies.

Until the day break, and the shadows flee away, turn, my beloved, and be thou like a roe or a young hart upon the mountains of Bether.

III

B Y night on my bed I sought him whom my soul loveth: I sought him, but I found him not.

I will rise now, and go about the city in the streets, and in the broad ways I will seek him whom my soul loveth: I sought him, but I found him not.

The watchmen that go about the city found me: to whom I said, Saw ye him whom my soul loveth?

It was but a little that I passed from them, but I found him whom my soul loveth: I held him, and would not let him go, until I had brought him into my mother's house, and into the chamber of her that conceived me.

I charge you, O ye daughters of Jerusalem, by the roes, and by the hinds of the field, that ye stir not up, nor awake my love, till he please.

Who is this that cometh out of the wilderness like pillars of smoke, perfumed with myrrh and frankincense, with all powders of the merchant?

Behold his bed, which is Solomon's; threescore valiant men are about it, of the valiant of Israel.

They all hold swords, being expert in war: every man hath his sword upon his thigh because of fear in the night.

King Solomon made himself a chariot of the wood of Lebanon.

He made the pillars thereof of silver, the bottom thereof

of gold, the covering of it of purple, the midst thereof being paved with love, for the daughters of Jerusalem.

Go forth, O ye daughters of Zion, and behold king Solomon with the crown wherewith his mother crowned him in the day of his espousals, and in the day of the gladness of his heart.

IV

BEHOLD, thou art fair, my love; behold, thou art fair; thou hast doves' eyes within thy locks: thy hair is as a flock of goats, that appear from mount Gilead.

Thy teeth are like a flock of sheep that are even shorn, which came up from the washing; whereof every one bear twins, and none is barren among them.

Thy lips are like a thread of scarlet, and thy speech is comely: thy temples are like a piece of a pomegranate within thy locks.

Thy neck is like the tower of David builded for an armoury, whereon there hang a thousand bucklers, all shields of mighty men.

Thy two breasts are like two young roes that are twins, which feed among the lilies.

Until the day break, and the shadows flee away, I will get me to the mountain of myrrh, and to the hill of frankincense.

Thou art all fair, my love; there is no spot in thee.

Come with me from Lebanon, my spouse, with me from Lebanon: look from the top of Amana, from the top of Shenir and Hermon, from the lions' dens, from the mountains of the leopards.

Thou hast ravished my heart, my sister, my spouse; thou hast ravished my heart with one of thine eyes, with one chain of thy neck.

How fair is thy love, my sister, my spouse! how much better is thy love than wine! and the smell of thine ointments than all spices!

Thy lips, O my spouse, drop as the honeycomb: honey and milk are under thy tongue; and the smell of thy garments is like the smell of Lebanon.

A garden inclosed is my sister, my spouse; a spring shut up, a fountain sealed.

21

Thy plants are an orchard of pomegranates, with pleasant fruits; camphire, with spikenard,

Spikenard and saffron; calamus and cinnamon, with all trees of frankincense; myrrh and aloes, with all the chief spices:

A fountain of gardens, a well of living waters, and streams from Lebanon.

Awake, O north wind; and come, thou south; blow upon my garden, that the spices thereof may flow out. Let my beloved come into his garden, and eat his pleasant fruits.

V

I AM come into my garden, my sister, my spouse: I have gathered my myrrh with my spice; I have eaten my honeycomb with my honey; I have drunk my wine with my milk; eat, O friends; drink, yea, drink abundantly, O beloved.

I sleep, but my heart waketh: it is the voice of my beloved that knocketh, saying, Open to me, my sister, my love, my dove, my undefiled: for my head is filled with dew, and my locks with the drops of the night.

I have put off my coat; how shall I put it on? I have washed my feet; how shall I defile them?

My beloved put in his hand by the hole of the door, and my bowels were moved for him.

I rose up to open to my beloved; and my hands dropped with myrrh, and my fingers with sweet smelling myrrh, upon the handles of the lock.

I opened to my beloved; but my beloved had withdrawn himself, and was gone: my soul failed when he spake: I sought him, but I could not find him; I called him, but he gave me no answer.

The watchmen that went about the city found me, they smote me, they wounded me; the keepers of the walls took away my veil from me.

I charge you, O daughters of Jerusalem, if ye find my beloved, that ye tell him, that I am sick of love.

What is thy beloved more than another beloved, O thou fairest among women? what is thy beloved more than another beloved, that thou dost so charge us?

My beloved is white and ruddy, the chiefest among ten thousand.

His head is as the most fine gold, his locks are bushy, and black as a raven.

His eyes are as the eyes of doves by the rivers of waters, washed with milk, and fitly set.

His cheeks are as a bed of spices, as sweet flowers : his lips like lilies, dropping sweet smelling myrrh.

His hands are as gold rings set with the beryl : his belly is as bright ivory overlaid with sapphires.

His legs are as pillars of marble, set upon sockets of fine gold : his countenance is as Lebanon, excellent as the cedars.

His mouth is most sweet : yea, he is altogether lovely. This is my beloved, and this is my friend, O daughters of Jerusalem.

VI

WHITHER is thy beloved gone, O thou fairest among women ? whither is thy beloved turned aside ? that we may seek him with thee.

My beloved is gone down into his garden, to the beds of spices, to feed in the gardens, and to gather lilies.

I am my beloved's, and my beloved is mine : he feedeth among the lilies.

Thou art beautiful, O my love, as Tirzah, comely as Jerusalem, terrible as an army with banners.

Turn away thine eyes from me, for they have overcome me : thy hair is as a flock of goats that appear from Gilead.

Thy teeth are as a flock of sheep which go up from the washing, whereof every one beareth twins, and there is not one barren among them.

As a piece of a pomegranate are thy temples within thy locks.

There are threescore queens, and fourscore concubines, and virgins without number.

My dove, my undefiled is but one ; she is the only one of her mother, she is the choice one of her that bare her. The daughters saw her, and blessed her ; yea, the queens and the concubines, and they praised her.

Who is she that looketh forth as the morning, fair as the moon, clear as the sun, and terrible as an army with banners ?

I went down into the garden of nuts to see the fruits of the valley, and to see whether the vine flourished, and the pomegranates budded.

Or ever I was aware, my soul made me like the chariots of Ammi-nadib.

Return, return, O Shulamite; return, return, that we may look upon thee. What will ye see in the Shulamite? As it were the company of two armies.

VII

H O W beautiful are thy feet with shoes, O prince's daughter! the joints of thy thighs are like jewels, the work of the hands of a cunning workman.

Thy navel is like a round goblet, which wanteth not liquor: thy belly is like an heap of wheat set about with lilies.

Thy two breasts are like two young roes that are twins.

Thy neck is as a tower of ivory; thine eyes like the fish-pools in Heshbon, by the gate of Bath-rabbim: thy nose is as the tower of Lebanon which looketh towards Damascus.

Thine head upon thee is like Carmel, and the hair of thine head like purple; the king is held in the galleries.

How fair and how pleasant art thou, O love, for delights!

This thy stature is like to a palm tree, and thy breasts to clusters of grapes.

I said, I will go up to the palm tree, I will take hold of the boughs thereof: now also thy breasts shall be as clusters of the vine, and the smell of thy nose like apples;

And the roof of thy mouth like the best wine for my beloved, that goeth down sweetly, causing the lips of those that are asleep to speak.

I am my beloved's, and his desire is toward me.

Come, my beloved, let us go forth into the field; let us lodge in the villages.

Let us get up early to the vineyards; let us see if the vine flourish, whether the tender grape appear, and the pomegranates bud forth: there will I give thee my loves.

The mandrakes give a smell, and at our gates are all manner of pleasant fruits, new and old, which I have laid up for thee, O my beloved.

24

VIII

O THAT thou wert as my brother, that sucked the breasts of my mother! when I should find thee without, I would kiss thee; yea, I should not be despised.

I would lead thee, and bring thee into my mother's house, who would instruct me: I would cause thee to drink of spiced wine of the juice of my pomegranate.

His left hand should be under my head, and his right hand should embrace me.

I charge you, O daughters of Jerusalem that ye stir not up, nor awake my love, until he please.

Who is this that cometh up from the wilderness, leaning upon her beloved? I raised thee up under the apple tree: there thy mother brought thee forth: there she brought thee forth that bare thee.

Set me as a seal upon thine heart, as a seal upon thine arm: for love is strong as death; jealousy is cruel as the grave: the coals thereof are coals of fire, which hath a most vehement flame

Many waters cannot quench love, neither can the floods drown it: if a man would give all the substance of his house for love, it would utterly be contemned.

We have a little sister, and she hath no breasts: what shall we do for our sister in the day when she shall be spoken for?

If she be a wall, we will build upon her a palace of silver: and if she be a door, we will inclose her with boards of cedar.

I am a wall, and my breasts like towers: then was I in his eyes as one that found favour.

Solomon had a vineyard at Baal-hamon; he let out the vineyard unto keepers; everyone for the fruit thereof was to bring a thousand pieces of silver.

My vineyard, which is mine, is before me: thou, O Solomon, must have a thousand, and those that keep the fruit thereof two hundred.

Thou that dwellest in the gardens, the companions hearken to thy voice; cause me to hear it.

Make haste, my beloved, and be thou like to a roe or to a young hart upon the mountains of spices.

Authorised Version.

TOM OF BEDLAM'S SONG

F R O M the hag and hungry goblin
That into rags would rend ye,
   All the spirits that stand
   By the naked man
In the book of moons, defend ye,

That of your five sound senses
You never be forsaken,
   Nor wander from
   Yourselves with Tom
Abroad to beg your bacon.

With a thought I took for Maudlin,
And a cruse of cockle pottage,
   With a thing thus tall,
   Sky bless you all,
I befell into this dotage.

I slept not since the Conquest,
Till then I never wakéd,
   Till the roguish boy
   Of love where I lay
Me found and stript me naked.

The moon's my constant mistress,
And the lonely owl my marrow ;
   The flaming drake
   And the night-crow make
Me music to my sorrow.

I know more than Apollo,
For oft, when he lies sleeping,
   I see the stars
   At mortal wars
In the wounded welkin weeping,

The moon embrace her shepherd,
And the queen of love her warrior,
   While the first doth horn
   The star of morn,
And the next the heavenly farrier.

With an host of furious fancies,
Whereof I am commander,
   With a burning spear
   And a horse of air
To the wilderness I wander ;

By a knight of ghosts and shadows
I summoned am to tourney
   Ten leagues beyond
   The wide world's end—
Methinks it is no journey.

Anonymous.

THERE IS A LADY SWEET AND KIND

THERE is a Lady sweet and kind,
Was never face so pleas'd my mind ;
I did but see her passing by,
And yet I love her till I die.

Her gesture, motion, and her smiles,
Her wit, her voice my heart beguiles,
Beguiles my heart, I know not why,
And yet I love her till I die.

Cupid is winged and doth range,
Her country so my love doth change :
But change she earth, or change she sky,
Yet will I love her till I die.

Anonymous.

LOVE NOT ME FOR COMELY GRACE

LOVE not me for comely grace,
   For my pleasing eye or face,
Nor for any outward part,
No, nor for a constant heart :
   For these may fail or turn to ill,
   So thou and I shall sever :
Keep, therefore, a true woman's eye,
And love me still but know not why—
   So hast thou the same reason still
   To doat upon me ever !

Anonymous.

27

THE CONCLUSION

E V E N such is Time, that takes in trust
  Our youth, our joys, our all we have,
And pays us but with earth and dust;
  Who, in the dark and silent grave,
When we have wandered all our ways,
Shuts up the story of our days.
But from this earth, this grave, this dust,
My God shall raise me up, I trust.

Walter Raleigh.

A FAREWELL TO ARMS

M Y golden locks Time hath to silver turn'd;
  O Time too swift, O swiftness never ceasing!
My youth 'gainst age, and age 'gainst time, hath
    spurn'd,
  But spurn'd in vain; youth waneth by increasing:
Beauty, strength, youth, are flowers but fading seen;
Duty, faith, love, are roots, and ever green.

My helmet now shall make an hive for bees,
  And lover's sonnets turn to holy psalms;
A man-at-arms must now serve on his knees,
  And feed on prayers, which are old age his alms:
But though from court to cottage I depart,
My saint is sure of my unspotted heart.

And when I saddest sit in homely cell,
  I'll teach my swains this carol for a song,—
" Blest be the hearts that wish my sovereign well,
  Curst be the souls that think her any wrong! "
Goddess, allow this aged man his right
To be your beadsman now that was your knight.

George Peele.

THE PARTING

S I N C E there's no help, come, let us kiss and part—
Nay, I have done, you get no more of me;
And I am glad, yea glad with all my heart,
That thus so cleanly I myself can free.
Shake hands for ever, cancel all our vows,

And, when we meet at any time again,
Be it not seen in either of our brows
That we one jot of former love retain.
Now at the last gasp of Love's latest breath,
When, his pulse failing, Passion speechless lies,
When Faith is kneeling by his bed of death,
And Innocence is closing up his eyes—
    Now if thou wouldst, when all have given him over,
    From death to life thou might'st him yet recover.

Michael Drayton.

TO THE SHADOW

LETTERS and lines we see are soon defaced,
Metals do waste and fret with canker's rust,
The diamond shall once consume to dust,
And freshest colours with foul stains disgraced ;
Paper and ink can paint but naked words,
To write with blood of force offends the sight,
And, if with tears, I find them all too light,
And sighs and signs a silly hope affords :
O sweetest Shadow, how thou serv'st my turn !
Which still shalt be, as long as there is sun,
Nor, whilst the world is, never shall be done,
Whilst moon shall shine, or any fire shall burn :
That everything whence shadow doth proceed,
May in his shadow my love's story read.

Michael Drayton.

SPRING AND WINTER

I

WHEN daisies pied and violets blue,
    And lady-smocks all silver-white,
And cuckoo-buds of yellow hue
    Do paint the meadows with delight,
The cuckoo then, on every tree,
Mocks married men ; for thus sings he,
            Cuckoo !
Cuckoo, cuckoo !—O word of fear.
Unpleasing to a married ear !

29

When shepherds pipe on oaten straws,
    And merry larks are ploughmen's clocks,
When turtles tread, and rooks, and daws,
    And maidens bleach their summer smocks
The cuckoo then, on every tree,
Mocks married men ; for thus sings he,
        Cuckoo !
Cuckoo, cuckoo !—O word of fear,
Unpleasing to a married ear !

        II

When icicles hang by the wall,
    And Dick the shepherd blows his nail,
And Tom bears logs into the hall,
    And milk comes frozen home in pail,
When blood is nipp'd, and ways be foul,
Then nightly sings the staring owl,
        To-whit !
To-who !—a merry note,
While greasy Joan doth keel the pot.

When all aloud the wind doth blow,
    And coughing drowns the parson's saw,
And birds sit brooding in the snow,
    And Marian's nose looks red and raw,
When roasted crabs hiss in the bowl,
Then nightly sings the staring owl,
        To-whit !
To-who !—a merry note,
While greasy Joan doth keel the pot.

William Shakespeare.

SONNET

LXV

SINCE brass, nor stone, nor earth, nor boundless sea,
But sad mortality o'ersways their power,
How with this rage shall beauty hold a plea,
Whose action is no stronger than a flower ?
O, how shall summer's honey breath hold out
Against the wreckful siege of battering days,
When rocks impregnable are not so stout,
Nor gates of steel so strong, but time decays ?
O fearful meditation ! where, alack,
Shall Time's best jewel from Time's quest lie hid ?

Or what strong hand can hold his swift foot back?
Or who his spoil of beauty can forbid?
   O, none, unless this miracle have might,
   That in black ink my love may still shine bright.

W. Shakespeare.

SONNET
CXXIX

T H E expense of spirit in a waste of shame
Is lust in action; and till action, lust
Is perjured, murderous, bloody, full of blame,
Savage, extreme, rude, cruel, not to trust,
Enjoy'd no sooner but despised straight,
Past reason hunted, and no sooner had
Past reason hated, as a swallow'd bait
On purpose laid to make the taker mad;
Mad in pursuit and in possession so;
Had, having, and in quest to have, extreme;
A bliss in proof, and proved, a very woe;
Before, a joy proposed; behind, a dream.
   All this the world well knows; yet none knows well
   To shun the heaven that leads men to this hell.

W. Shakespeare.

SONNET
CXXX

M Y mistress' eyes are nothing like the sun;
Coral is far more red than her lips red;
If snow be white, why then her breasts are dun;
If hairs be wires, black wires grow in her head.
I have seen roses damask'd, red and white,
But no such roses see I in her cheeks;
And in some perfumes is there more delight
Than in the breath that from my mistress reeks.
I love to hear her speak, yet well I know
That music hath a far more pleasing sound;
I grant I never saw a goddess go;
My mistress, when she walks, treads on the ground:
   And yet, by heaven, I think my love as rare
   As any she belied with false compare.

W. Shakespeare.

31

SPRING

SPRING, the sweet Spring, is the year's pleasant king
Then blooms each thing, then maids dance in a ring,
Cold doth not sting, the pretty birds do sing—
    Cuckoo, jug-jug, pu-we, to-witta-woo!

The palm and may make country houses gay,
Lambs frisk and play, the shepherds pipe all day,
And we hear aye birds tune this merry lay—
    Cuckoo, jug-jug, pu-we, to-witta woo!

The fields breathe sweet, the daisies kiss our feet,
Young lovers meet, old wives a-sunning sit,
In every street these tunes our ears do greet—
    Cuckoo, jug-jug, pu-we, to-witta-woo!
      Spring, the sweet Spring!

Thomas Nashe.

IN TIME OF PESTILENCE

ADIEU, farewell earth's bliss!
This world uncertain is:
Fond are life's lustful joys,
Death proves them all but toys.
None from his darts can fly;
I am sick, I must die—
    Lord, have mercy on us!

Rich men, trust not in wealth,
Gold cannot buy you health;
Physic himself must fade;
All things to end are made;
The plague full swift goes by;
I am sick, I must die—
    Lord, have mercy on us!

Beauty is but a flower
Which wrinkles will devour;
Brightness falls from the air;
Queens have died young and fair;
Dust hath clos'd Helen's eye;
I am sick, I must die—
    Lord, have mercy on us!

Strength stoops unto the grave,
Worms feed on Hector brave;
Swords may not fight with fate;
Earth still holds ope her gate;
Come, come! the bells do cry;
I am sick, I must die—
    Lord, have mercy on us!

Wit with his wantonness
Tasteth death's bitterness;
Hell's executioner
Hath no ears for to hear
What vain art can reply;
I am sick, I must die—
    Lord, have mercy on us!

Haste therefore each degree
To welcome destiny;
Heaven is our heritage,
Earth but a player's stage.
Mount we unto the sky;
I am sick, I must die—
    Lord, have mercy on us!

Thomas Nashe.

KIND ARE HER ANSWERS

KIND are her answers,
  But her performance keeps no day;
Breaks time, as dancers
  From their own music when they stray:
  All her free favours
And smooth words wing my hopes in vain.
O did ever voice so sweet but only feign?
  Can true love yield such delay,
  Converting joy to pain?

Lost is our freedom,
  When we submit to women so:
Why do we need them,
  When in their best they work our woe?
  There is no wisdom

C

Can alter ends, by Fate prefixed.
O why is the good of man with evil mixed ?
   Never were days yet call'd two,
   But one night went betwixt.

Thomas Campion.

THE TRIUMPH

SEE the Chariot at hand here of Love,
   Wherein my Lady rideth !
Each that draws is a swan or a dove,
   And well the car Love guideth.
As she goes, all hearts do duty
     Unto her beauty ;
And enamour'd do wish, so they might
     But enjoy such a sight,
That they still were to run by her side,
Through swords, through seas, whither she would ride.

Do but look on her eyes, they do light
   All that Love's world compriseth !
Do but look on her hair, it is bright
   As Love's star when it riseth !
Do but mark, her forehead's smoother
     Than words that soothe her ;
And from her arch'd brows such a grace
     Sheds itself through the face,
As alone there triumphs to the life
All the gain, all the good, of the elements' strife.

Have you seen but a bright lily grow
   Before rude hands have touch'd it ?
Have you mark'd but the fall of the snow
   Before the soil hath smutch'd it ?
Have you felt the wool of beaver,
     Or swan's down ever ?
Or have smelt of the bud of the brier,
     Or the nard in the fire ?
Or have tasted the bag of the bee ?
O so white, O so soft, O so sweet is she !

Ben Jonson.

34

THE GOOD-MORROW

I WONDER, by my troth, what thou and I
Did, till we loved ? were we not wean'd till then ?
But suck'd on country pleasures, childishly ?
Or snorted we in the Seven Sleepers' den ?
'Twas so ; but this, all pleasures fancies be ;
If ever any beauty I did see,
Which I desired, and got, 'twas but a dream of thee,

And now good-morrow to our waking souls,
Which watch not one another out of fear ;
For love all love of other sights controls,
And makes one little room an everywhere.
Let sea-discoverers to new worlds have gone ;
Let maps to other worlds on worlds have shown ;
Let us possess one world ; each hath one, and is one.

My face in thine eye, thine in mine appears,
And true plain hearts do in the faces rest ;
Where can we find two better hemispheres
Without sharp north, without declining west ?
Whatever dies, was not mix'd equally ;
If our two loves be one, or thou and I
Love so alike that none can slacken, none can die.

John Donne.

THE SUN RISING

BUSY old fool, unruly Sun,
        Why dost thou thus,
Through windows, and through curtains, call on us ?
Must to thy motions lovers' seasons run ?
        Saucy pedantic wretch, go chide
        Late school-boys and sour prentices,
    Go tell court-huntsmen that the king will ride,
    Call country ants to harvest offices ;
Love, all alike, no season knows nor clime,
Nor hours, days, months, which are the rags of time.

        Thy beams so reverend and strong
        Why shouldst thou think ?
I could eclipse and cloud them with a wink,
But that I would not lose her sight so long.

35

If her eyes have not blinded thine,
　Look, and to-morrow late tell me,
　Whether both th' Indias of spice and mine
Be where thou left'st them, or lie here with me.
Ask for those kings whom thou saw'st yesterday,
And thou shalt hear, " All here in one bed lay."
　　She's all states, and all princes I ;
　　Nothing else is ;
Princes do but play us ; compared to this,
All honour's mimic, all wealth alchemy.
　　Thou, Sun, art half as happy as we,
　　In that the world's contracted thus ;
　Thine age asks ease, and since thy duties be
To warm the world, that's done in warming us.
Shine here to us, and thou art everywhere ;
This bed thy centre is, these walls thy sphere.

John Donne.

LOVE'S DEITY

I LONG to talk with some old lover's ghost,
　Who died before the god of love was born.
I cannot think that he, who then loved most,
　　Sunk so low as to love one which did scorn.
But since this god produced a destiny,
And that vice-nature, custom, lets it be,
　I must love her that loves not me.

Sure, they which made him god, meant not so much,
　Nor he in his young godhead practised it.
But when an even flame two hearts did touch,
　His office was indulgently to fit
Actives to passives. Correspondency
Only his subject was ; it cannot be
　Love, till I love her, who loves me.

But every modern god will now extend
　His vast prerogative as far as Jove.
To rage, to lust, to write to, to commend,
　All is the purlieu of the god of love.

O ! were we waken'd by this tyranny
To ungod this child again, it could not be
   I should love her, who loves not me.

Rebel and atheist too, why murmur I,
   As though I felt the worst that love could do ?
Love might make me leave loving, or might try
   A deeper plague, to make her love me too ;
Which, since she loves before, I'm loth to see.
Falsehood is worse than hate ; and that must be,
   If she whom I love, should love me.

                           John Donne.

THE DREAM

DEAR love, for nothing less than thee
Would I have broke this happy dream ;
      It was a theme
For reason, much too strong for fantasy.
Therefore thou waked'st me wisely ; yet
My dream thou brokest not, but continued'st it.
Thou art so true that thoughts of thee suffice
To make dreams truths, and fables histories ;
Enter these arms, for since thou thought'st it best,
Not to dream all my dream, let's act the rest.

As lightning, or a taper's light,
Thine eyes, and not thy noise waked me ;
      Yet I thought thee
—For thou lov'st truth—an angel, at first sight ;
But when I saw thou saw'st my heart,
And knew'st my thoughts beyond an angel's art,
When thou knew'st what I dreamt, when thou knew'st
Excess of joy would wake me, and camest then, [when
I must confess, it could not choose but be
Profane, to think thee any thing but thee.

Coming and staying show'd thee, thee,
But rising makes me doubt, that now
      Thou art not thou.
That love is weak where fear's as strong as he ;
'Tis not all spirit, pure and brave,
If mixture it of fear, shame, honour have ;

37

Perchance as torches, which must ready be,
Men light and put out, so thou deal'st with me;
Thou cam'st to kindle, go'st to come; then I
Will dream that hope again, but else would die.

John Donne.

LOVE'S GROWTH

I SCARCE believe my love to be so pure
    As I had thought it was,
    Because it doth endure
Vicissitude, and season, as the grass;
Methinks I lied all winter, when I swore
My love was infinite, if spring make it more.

But if this medicine, love, which cures all sorrow
    With more, not only be no quintessence,
    But mix'd of all stuffs, vexing soul, or sense,
And of the sun his active vigour borrow,
Love's not so pure, and abstract as they use
To say, which have no mistress but their Muse;
But as all else, being elemented too,
Love sometimes would contemplate, sometimes do.

And yet no greater, but more eminent,
    Love by the spring is grown;
    As in the firmament
Stars by the sun are not enlarged, but shown,
Gentle love deeds, as blossoms on a bough,
From love's awaken'd root do bud out now.

If, as in water stirr'd more circles be
    Produced by one, love such additions take,
    Those like so many spheres but one heaven make,
For they are all concentric unto thee;
And though each spring do add to love new heat,
As princes do in times of action get
New taxes, and remit them not in peace,
No winter shall abate this spring's increase.

John Donne.

THE ECSTACY

WHERE, like a pillow on a bed,
   A pregnant bank swell'd up, to rest
The violet's reclining head,
   Sat we two, one another's best.

Our hands were firmly cemented
   By a fast balm, which thence did spring ;
Our eye-beams twisted, and did thread
   Our eyes upon one double string.

So to engraft our hands, as yet
   Was all the means to make us one ;
And pictures in our eyes to get
   Was all our propagation.

As, 'twixt two equal armies, Fate
   Suspends uncertain victory,
Our souls—which to advance their state,
   Were gone out—hung 'twixt her and me.

And whilst our souls negotiate there,
   We like sepulchral statues lay ;
All day, the same our postures were,
   And we said nothing, all the day.

If any, so by love refined,
   That he soul's language understood,
And by good love were grown all mind,
   Within convenient distance stood,

He—though he knew not which soul spake,
   Because both meant, both spake the same—
Might thence a new concoction take,
   And part far purer than he came.

This ecstacy doth unperplex
   (We said) and tell us what we love ;
We see by this, it was not sex ;
   We see, we saw not, what did move :

But as all several souls contain
   Mixture of things they know not what,
Love these mix'd souls doth mix again,
   And makes both one, each this and that.

A single violet transplant,
　　The strength, the colour, and the size—
All which before was poor and scant—
　　Redoubles still, and multiplies.

When love with one another so
　　Interinanimates two souls,
That abler soul, which thence doth flow,
　　Defects of loneliness controls.

We then, who are this new soul, know,
　　Of what we are composed and made,
For th'atomies of which we grow
　　Are souls, whom no change can invade.

But, O alas ! so long, so far,
　　Our bodies why do we forbear ?
They are ours, though they're not we ; we are
　　Th'intelligences, they the spheres.

We owe them thanks, because they thus
　　Did us, to us, at first convey,
Yielded their forces, sense, to us,
　　Nor are dross to us, but allay.

On man heaven's influence works not so,
　　But that it first imprints the air ;
So soul into the soul may flow,
　　Though it to body first repair.

As our blood labours to beget
　　Spirits, as like souls as it can ;
Because such fingers need to knit
　　That subtle knot, which makes us man ;

So must pure lovers' souls descend
　　To affections, and to faculties,
Which sense may reach and apprehend,
　　Else a great prince in prison lies.

To our bodies turn we then, that so
　　Weak men on love reveal'd may look ;
Love's mysteries in souls do grow,
　　But yet the body is his book.

And if some lover, such as we,
   Have heard this dialogue of one,
Let him still mark us, he shall see
   Small change when we're to bodies gone.
John Donne.

DIVINE POEM

BATTER my heart, three personed God; for you
As yet but knock, breathe, shine, and seek to mend.
That I may rise and stand, o'erthrow me and bend
Your force to break, blow, burn and make me new.
I, like an usurped town, to another due,
Labour to admit you, but Oh, to no end ;
Reason, your viceroy in me, me should defend,
But is captived and proves weak or untrue.
Yet dearly I love you and would be loved fain,
But am betrothed unto your enemy :
Divorce me, untie or break that knot again,
Take me to you, imprison me, for I
Except you enthrall me, never shall be free,
Nor ever chaste, except you ravish me.
John Donne.

GOD LYÆUS

   GOD LYÆUS, ever young,
   Ever honour'd, ever sung,
   Stain'd with blood of lusty grapes,
   In a thousand lusty shapes
   Dance upon the mazer's brim,
   In the crimson liquor swim ,
   From thy plenteous hand divine
   Let a river run with wine :
      God of youth, let this day here
      Enter neither care nor fear.
John Fletcher.

OBERON'S FEAST

SHAPCOT! to thee the Fairy State
I with discretion, dedicate.
Because thou prizest things that are
Curious and unfamiliar,

C*

Take first the feast ; these dishes gone,
We'll see the Fairy Court anon.
A little mushroom-table spread,
After short prayers, they set on bread ;
A moon-parch'd grain of purest wheat,
With some small glittering grit, to eat
His choice bits with ; then in a trice
They make a feast less great than nice.
But all this while his eye is serv'd,
We must not think his ear was starv'd
But that there was in place to stir
His spleen, the chirring Grasshopper ;
The merry Cricket, puling Fly,
The piping Gnat for minstrelsy.
And now, we must imagine first,
The Elves present to quench his thirst
A pure seed-pearl of infant dew,
Brought and besweetened in a blue
And pregnant violet ; which done,
His kitling eyes begin to run
Quite through the table, where he spies
The horns of papery Butterflies :
Of which he eats, and tastes a little
Of that we call the cuckoo's spittle.
A little fuzz-ball pudding stands
By, yet not blessed by his hands,
That was too coarse ; but then forthwith
He ventures boldly on the pith
Of sugared rush, and eats the sag
And well bestrutted Bee's sweet bag :
Gladding his palate with some store
Of Emit's eggs ; what would he more ?
But beards of Mice, a Newt's stew'd thigh,
A roasted Earwig, and a Fly ;
With the red-capp'd Worm, that's shut
Within the concave of a nut,
Brown as his tooth. A little Moth,
Late fattened in a piece of cloth :
With wither'd cherries ; Mandrake's ears ;
Mole's eyes ; to these, the slain Stag's tears
The unctuous dewlaps of a Snail ;

The broke heart of a Nightingale
O'ercome in music; with a wine,
Ne'er ravish'd from the flattering vine,
But gently press'd from the soft side
Of the most sweet and dainty bride,
Brought in a dainty daisy, which
He fully quaffs up to bewitch
His blood to height; this done, commended
Grace by his Priest : *The feast is ended.*

Robert Herrick.

EXEQUY ON HIS WIFE

ACCEPT, thou shrine of my dead saint,
Instead of dirges this complaint;
And for sweet flowers to crown thy hearse
Receive a strew of weeping verse
From thy grieved Friend, whom thou might'st
      see
Quite melted into tears for thee.
   Dear loss ! since thy untimely fate,
My task hath been to meditate
On thee, on thee ! Thou are the book,
The library whereon I look,
Tho' almost blind. For thee, loved clay,
I languish out, not live, the day,
Using no other exercise
But what I practise with mine eyes :
By which wet glasses I find out
How lazily time creeps about
To one that mourns : this, only this,
My exercise and business is :
So I compute the weary hours,
With sighs dissolved into showers.
No wonder if my time go thus
Backward and most preposterous;
Thou hast benighted me ; thy set
This eve of blackness did beget,
Who wast my day (tho' overcast
Before thou hadst thy noontide past) :
And I remember must in tears

43

Thou scarce hadst seen so many years
As day tells hours. By thy clear sun
My love and fortune first did run;
But thou wilt never more appear
Folded within my hemisphere,
Since both thy light and motion,
Like a fled star, is fall'n and gone,
And 'twixt me and my soul's dear wish
The earth now interposed is,
Which such a strange eclipse doth make
As ne'er was read in Almanack.
   I could allow thee for a time
To darken me and my sad clime;
Were it a month, a year, or ten,
I would thy exile live till then,
And all that space my mirth adjourn—
So thou wouldst promise to return,
And putting off thy ashy shroud
At length disperse this sorrow's cloud.
   But woe is me ! the longest date
Too narrow is to calculate
These empty hopes : never shall I
Be so much blest as to descry
A glimpse of thee, till that day come
Which shall the earth to cinders doom,
And a fierce fever must calcine
The body of this world—like thine,
My little world ! That fit of fire
Once off, our bodies shall aspire
To our soul's bliss : then we shall rise
And view ourselves with clearer eyes
In that calm region where no night
Can hide us from each other's sight.
   Meantime thou hast her, earth : much good
May my harm do thee ! Since it stood
With Heaven's will I might not call
Her longer mine, I give thee all
My short-lived right and interest
In her whom living I loved best :
With a most free and bounteous grief
I give thee what I could not keep.

44

Be kind to her, and prithee look
Thou write into thy Doomsday book
Each parcel of this rarity
Which in thy casket shrin'd doth lie :
See that thou make thy reck'ning straight,
And yield her back again by weight;
For thou must audit on thy trust
Each grain and atom of this dust
As thou wilt answer Him that lent—
Not gave—thee my dear monument.
So close the ground, and 'bout her shade
Black curtains draw ; my bride is laid.

   Sleep on, my Love, in thy cold bed
Never to be disquieted !
My last good night ! Thou wilt not wake
Till I thy fate shall overtake :
Till age, or grief, or sickness must
Marry my body to that dust
It so much loves ; and fill the room
My heart keeps empty in thy tomb.
Stay for me there : I will not fail
To meet thee in that hollow vale,
And think not much of my delay :
I am already on the way,
And follow thee with all the speed
Desire can make, or sorrows breed.
Each minute is a short degree
And every hour a step towards thee.
At night when I betake to rest,
Next morn I rise nearer my West
Of life, almost by eight hours' sail,
Than when sleep breath'd his drowsy gale.

   Thus from the Sun my bottom steers
And my day's compass downward bears :
Nor labour I to stem the tide
Through which to thee I swiftly glide.
   'Tis true—with shame and grief I yield—
Thou, like the van, first took'st the field ;
And gotten hast the victory
In thus adventuring to die
Before me, whose more years might crave

A just precedence in the grave.
But hark ! my pulse, like a soft drum,
Beats my approach, tells thee I come ;
And slow howe'er my marches be
I shall at last sit down by thee.
The thought of this bids me go on
And wait my dissolution
With hope and comfort. Dear—forgive
The crime—I am content to live
Divided, with but half a heart,
Till we shall meet and never part.

Henry King.

THE PULLEY

WHEN God at first made man,
Having a glass of blessings standing by—
Let us (said he) pour on him all we can ;
Let the world's riches, which dispersed lie,
   Contract into a span.

So strength first made a way,
Then beauty flow'd, then wisdom, honour, pleasure :
When almost all was out, God made a stay,
Perceiving that, alone of all His treasure,
   Rest in the bottom lay.

For if I should (said he)
Bestow this jewel also on My creature,
He would adore My gifts instead of Me,
And rest in Nature, not the God of Nature :
   So both should losers be.

Yet let him keep the rest,
But keep them with repining restlessness ;
Let him be rich and weary, that at least,
If goodness lead him not, yet weariness
   May toss him to my breast.

George Herbert.

46

DISCIPLINE

THROW away thy rod,
Throw away thy wrath;
   O my God,
Take the gentle path.

For my heart's desire
Unto thine is bent;
   I aspire
To a full consent.

Not a word or look
I affect to own,
   But by book,
And thy book alone.

Though I fail, I weep;
Though I halt in pace,
   Yet I creep
To the throne of grace.

Then let wrath remove,
Love will do the deed;
   For with love
Stony hearts will bleed.

Love is swift of foot;
Love's a man of war,
   And can shoot,
And can hit from far.

Who can 'scape his bow?
That which wrought on thee,
   Brought thee low,
Needs must work on me.

Throw away thy rod:
Though man frailties hath,
   Thou art God;
Throw away thy wrath.

George Herbert.

SONG

ASK me no more where Jove bestows,
When June is past, the fading rose;
For in your beauty's orient deep
These flowers, as in their causes, sleep.

Ask me no more whither do stray
The golden atoms of the day;
For in pure love heaven did prepare
Those powders to enrich your hair.

Ask me no more whither doth haste
The nightingale when May is past;
For in your sweet dividing throat
She winters and keeps warm her note.

Ask me no more where those stars 'light
That downwards fall in dead of night;
For in your eyes they sit, and there
Fixèd become as in their sphere.

Ask me no more if east or west
The phœnix builds her spicy nest;
For unto you at last she flies,
And in your fragrant bosom dies.

Thomas Carew.

A DEVOUT LOVER

I HAVE a mistress, for perfections rare
In every eye, but in my thoughts most fair.
Like tapers on the altar shine her eyes;
Her breath is the perfume of sacrifice;
And whersoe'er my fancy would begin,
Still her perfection lets religion in.
We sit and talk, and kiss away the hours
As chastely as the morning dews kiss flowers:
I touch her, like my beads, with devout care,
And come unto my courtship as my prayer.

Thomas Randolph.

48

WHY SO PALE AND WAN?

WHY so pale and wan, fond lover?
    Prithee, why so pale?
Will when looking well can't move her,
    Looking ill prevail?
    Prithee, why so pale?

Why so dull and mute, young sinner?
    Prithee, why so mute?
Will, when speaking well can't win her,
    Saying nothing do 't?
    Prithee, why so mute?

Quit, quit for shame! This will not move;
    This cannot take her.
If of herself she will not love,
    Nothing can make her;
    The devil take her!

John Suckling.

UPON A WEDDING

I TELL thee, Dick, where I have been,
Where I the rarest things have seen;
    O, things without compare!
Such sights again cannot be found
In any place on English ground,
    Be it at wake or fair.

At Charing Cross, hard by the way,
Where we, thou know'st, do sell our hay,
    There is a house with stairs;
And there did I see coming down
Such folk as are not in our town,
    Forty at least, in pairs.

Amongst the rest, one pest'lent fine
(His beard no bigger though than thine)
    Walked on before the rest:
Our landlord looks like nothing to him:
The King (God bless him) 'twould undo him,
    Should he go still so drest.

At Course-a-Park, without all doubt,
He should have first been taken out
    By all the maids i' th' town:
Though lusty Roger there had been,
Or little George upon the Green,
    Or Vincent of the Crown.

But wot you what? the youth was going
To make an end of all his wooing;
    The parson for him stay'd:
Yet by his leave, for all his haste,
He did not so much wish all past,
    Perchance, as did the maid.

The maid (and thereby hangs a tale),
For such a maid no Whitsun-ale
    Could ever yet produce:
No grape, that's kindly ripe, could be
So round, so plump, so soft as she,
    Nor half so full of juice.

Her finger was so small, the ring
Would not stay on, which they did bring,
    It was too wide a peck:
And to say truth (for out it must)
It looked like the great collar, just,
    About our young colt's neck.

Her feet beneath her petticoat,
Like little mice, stole in and out,
    As if they fear'd the light:
But O she dances such a way!
No sun upon an Easter-day
    Is half so fine a sight.

He would have kissed her once or twice,
But she would not, she was so nice,
    She would not do't in sight,
And then she looked as who should say:
I will do what I list to-day,
    And you shall do't at night.

Her cheeks so rare a white was on,
No daisy makes comparison,
    Who sees them is undone;
For streaks of red were mingled there
Such as are on a Catherine pear,
    The side that's next the sun.

Her lips were red, and one was thin,
Compar'd to that was next her chin
    (Some bee had stung it newly);
But, Dick, her eyes so guard her face;
I durst no more upon them gaze
    Than on the sun in July.

Her mouth so small, when she does speak,
Thou'dst swear her teeth her words did break,
    That they might passage get;
But she so handled still the matter,
They came as good as ours, or better,
    And are not spent a whit.

If wishing should be any sin,
The parson himself had guilty been,
    She look'd that day so purely;
And did the youth so oft the feat
At night, as some did in conceit,
    It would have spoiled him surely.

Just in the nick the cook knocked thrice,
And all the waiters in a trice
    His summons did obey;
Each serving-man, with dish in hand,
Marched boldly up, like our trained band,
    Presented, and away.

When all the meat was on the table,
What man of knife or teeth was able
    To stay to be intreated?
And this the very reason was,
Before the parson could say grace,
    The company was seated.

The business of the kitchen's great,
For it is fit that men should eat,
    Nor was it there denied—
Passion o' me, how I run on!
There's that that would be thought upon,
    I trow, besides the bride.

Now hats fly off, and youths carouse;
Healths first go round, and then the house,
    The bride's came thick and thick:
And when 'twas nam'd another's health,
Perhaps he made it hers by stealth;
    And who could help it, Dick?

On the sudden up they rise and dance;
Then sit again and sigh, and glance:
    Then dance again and kiss:
Thus several ways the time did pass,
Whilst ev'ry woman wished her place,
    And every man wished his.

By this time all were stol'n aside
To counsel and undress the bride;
    But that he must not know:
But yet 'twas thought he guess'd her mind,
And did not mean to stay behind
    Above an hour or so.

When in he came, Dick, there she lay
Like new-fall'n snow melting away
    ('Twas time, I trow, to part)
Kisses were now the only stay,
Which soon she gave, as who would say,
    God b' w' ye, with all my heart.

But, just as Heaven would have, to cross it,
In came the bridesmaids with the posset:
    The bridegroom ate in spite;
For had he left the women to 't,
It would have cost two hours to do 't,
    Which were too much that night.

At length the candle's out, and now
All that they had not done they do.
    What that is, who can tell?
But I believe it was no more
Than thou and I have done before
    With Bridget and with Nell.

John Suckling.

DRINKING

THE thirsty earth soaks up the rain,
And drinks and gapes for drink again;
The plants suck in the earth, and are
With constant drinking fresh and fair;
The sea itself (which one would think
Should have but little need of drink)
Drinks twice ten thousand rivers up,
So fill'd that they o'erflow the cup.
The busy Sun (and one would guess
By's drunken fiery face no less)
Drinks up the sea, and when he's done,
The Moon and Stars drink up the Sun:
They drink and dance by their own light,
They drink and revel all the night:
Nothing in Nature's sober found,
But an eternal health goes round.
Fill up the bowl, then, fill it high,
Fill all the glasses there—for why
Should every creature drink but I?
Why, man of morals, tell me why?

Abraham Cowley.

TO HIS COY MISTRESS

HAD we but world enough, and time,
This coyness, lady, were no crime.
We would sit down, and think which way
To walk, and pass our long love's day.
Thou by the Indian Ganges' side
Should'st rubies find : I by the tide
Of Humber would complain.   I would

53

Love you ten years before the Flood,
And you should, if you please, refuse
Till the conversion of the Jews.
My vegetable love should grow
Vaster than empires, and more slow.
An hundred years should go to praise
Thine eyes, and on thy forehead gaze :
Two hundred to adore each breast :
But thirty thousand to the rest ;
An age at least to every part,
And the last age should shew your heart.
For, lady, you deserve this state,
Nor would I love at lower rate.

But at my back I always hear
Time's wingèd chariot hurrying near :
And yonder all before us lie
Deserts of vast eternity.
Thy beauty shall no more be found ;
Nor, in thy marble vault, shall sound
My echoing song ; then worms shall try
That long-preserv'd virginity :
And your quaint honour turn to dust,
And into ashes all my lust.
The grave's a fine and private place,
But none, I think, do there embrace.

Now, therefore, while the youthful hue
Sits on thy skin like morning dew,
And while thy willing soul transpires
At every pore with instant fires,
Now let us sport us while we may ;
And now, like amorous birds of prey,
Rather at once our Time devour,
Than languish in his slow-chapt power.
Let us roll all our strength and all
Our sweetness up into one ball,
And tear our pleasures with rough strife
Through the iron gates of life.
Thus, though we cannot make our Sun
Stand still, yet we will make him run.

Andrew Marvell.

THE FAIR SINGER

T O make a final conquest of all me,
Love did compose so sweet an enemy,
In whom both beauties to my death agree,
Joining themselves in fatal harmony ;
That, while she with her eyes my heart does bind,
She with her voice might captivate my mind.

I could have fled from one but singly fair :
My disentangled soul itself might save,
Breaking the curled trammels of her hair.
But how should I avoid to be her slave,
Whose subtle art invisibly can wreathe
My fetters of the very air I breathe ?

It had been easy fighting in some plain,
Where victory might hang in equal choice,
But all resistance against her is vain,
Who has the advantage both of eyes and voice ;
And all my forces needs must be undone,
She having gained both the wind and sun.

Andrew Marvell.

THE GARDEN

H O W vainly men themselves amaze
To win the palm, the oak, or bays ;
And their incessant labours see
Crowned from some single herb, or tree,
Whose short and narrow-verged shade
Does prudently their toils upbraid ;
While all flow'rs and all trees do close
To weave the garlands of repose.

Fair Quiet, have I found thee here,
And Innocence, thy sister dear ?
Mistaken long, I sought you then
In busy companies of men.
Your sacred plants, if here below,
Only among the plants will grow ;
Society is all but rude
To this delicious solitude.

55

No white nor red was ever seen
So amorous as this lovely green.
Fond lovers, cruel as their flame,
Cut in these trees their mistress' name:
Little, alas! they know or heed
How far these beauties hers exceed!
Fair trees! wheres'e'er your barks I wound
No name shall but your own be found.

When we have run our passion's heat,
Love hither makes his best retreat.
The Gods, that mortal beauty chase,
Still in a tree did end their race;
Apollo hunted Daphne so,
Only that she might laurel grow;
And Pan did after Syrinx speed,
Not as a nymph, but for a reed.

What wondrous life is this I lead!
Ripe apples drop about my head;
The luscious clusters of the vine
Upon my mouth do crush their wine;
The nectaren, and curious peach,
Into my hands themselves do reach;
Stumbling on melons, as I pass,
Insnared with flowers, I fall on grass.

Meanwhile, the mind, from pleasure less,
Withdraws into its happiness:
The mind, that ocean where each kind
Does straight its own resemblance find;
Yet it creates, transcending these,
Far other worlds, and other seas;
Annihilating all that's made
To a green thought in a green shade.

Here at the fountain's sliding foot,
Or at some fruit-tree's mossy root,
Casting the body's vest aside,
My soul into the boughs does glide:

There like a bird it sits, and sings,
Then whets and claps its silver wings ;
And, till prepared for longer flight,
Waves in its plumes the various light.

Such was that happy garden-state,
While man there walked without a mate :
After a place so pure and sweet,
What other help could yet be meet !
But 'twas beyond a mortal's share
To wander solitary there :
Two paradises 'twere in one,
To live in paradise alone.

How well the skilful gardener drew
Of flowers, and herbs, this dial new ;
Where, from above, the milder sun
Does through a fragrant zodiac run ;
And, as it works, the industrious bee
Computes its time as well as we.
How could such sweet and wholesome hours
Be reckon'd but with herbs and flowers !

Andrew Marvell.

THE REVIVAL

UNFOLD, unfold ! take in his light,
Who makes thy cares more short than night.
The joys which with his day-star rise
He deals to all but drowsy eyes ;
And (what the men of this world miss)
Some drops and dews of future bliss.

Hark, how his winds have chang'd their note,
And with warm whispers call thee out.
The frosts are past, the storms are gone,
And backward life at last comes on.
The lofty groves in express joys
Reply unto the turtle's voice ;
And here in dust and dirt, O here
The lilies of his love appear !

Henry Vaughan.

57

THE ECLIPSE

WHITHER, O whither didst thou fly
When I did grieve thine holy eye
When thou didst mourn to see me lost,
And all thy care and counsels crost.
O do not grieve, where'er thou art !
Thy grief is an undoing smart,
Which doth not only pain, but break
My heart, and makes me blush to speak.
Thy anger I could kiss, and will :
But O thy grief, thy grief doth kill !

Henry Vaughan.

THE WORLD

I SAW Eternity the other night,
Like a great Ring of pure and endless light,
    All calm, as it was bright ;
And round beneath it, Time in hours, days, years,
    Driven by the spheres
Like a vast shadow moved ; in which the world
    And all her train were hurled.
The doting lover in his quaintest strain
    Did there complain ;
Near him, his lute, his fancy, and his flights,
    Wit's sour delights,
With gloves, and knots, the silly snares of pleasure,
    Yet his dear treasure,
All scattered lay, while he his eyes did pour
    Upon a flower.

The darksome statesman, hung with weights and woe,
Like a thick midnight-fog, moved there so slow,
    He did not stay, nor go ;
Condemning thoughts—like sad eclipses—scowl
    Upon his soul,
And clouds of crying witnesses without
    Pursu'd him with one shout.
Yet digg'd the mole, and lest his ways be found,
    Worked under ground,

Where he did clutch his prey ; (But one did see
    That policy) ;
Churches and altars fed him ; perjuries
    Were gnats and flies ;
It rained about him blood and tears ; but he
    Drank them as free.

The fearful miser on a heap of rust
Sate pining all his life there, did scarce trust
    His own hands with the dust,
Yet would not place one piece above, but lives
    In fear of thieves.
Thousands there were as frantic as himself
    And hugged each one his pelf,
The downright epicure placed heaven in sense
    And scorn'd pretence,
While others, slipp'd into a wide excess,
    Said little less ;
The weaker sort slight, trivial wares enslave,
    Who think them brave ;
And poor, despised Truth sate counting by
    Their victory.

Yet some, who all this while did weep and sing,
And sing, and weep, soared up into the Ring ;
    But most would use no wing.
O fools (said I) thus to prefer dark night
    Before true light !
To live in grots and caves, and hate the day
    Because it shows the way,
The way, which from this dead and dark abode
    Leads up to God,
A way where you might tread the sun, and be
    More bright than he.
But as I did their madness so discuss,
    One whisper'd thus,
This Ring the Bridegroom did for none provide,
    But for his bride.

                Henry Vaughan.

59

THE NIGHT

THROUGH that pure virgin-shrine,
That sacred veil drawn o'er thy glorious noon,
That men might look and live, as glow-worms shine
    And face the moon :
      Wise Nicodemus saw such light
      As made him know his God by night.

Most blest believer he !
Who in that land of darkness and blind eyes
Thy long-expected healing wings could see
    When thou didst rise,
      And, what can never more be done,
      Did at midnight speak with the Sun !

O who will tell me, where
He found thee at that dead and silent hour ?
What hallowed solitary ground did bear
    So rare a flower
      Within whose sacred leaves did lie
      The fulness of the Deity ?

No mercy-seat of gold,
No dead and dusty cherub, nor carved stone,
But his own living works did my Lord hold
    And lodge alone ;
      Where trees and herbs did watch and peep
      And wonder, while the Jews did sleep.

Dear Night ! this world's defeat ;
The stop to busy fools ; care's check and curb ;
The day of spirits ; my soul's calm retreat
    Which none disturb !
      Christ's progress, and his prayer-time ;
      The hours to which high Heaven doth chime.

God's silent, searching flight :
When my Lord's head is fill'd with dew and all
His locks are wet with the clear drops of night ;
    His still, soft call ;
      His knocking-time ; the soul's dumb watch,
      When spirits their fair kindred catch.

Were all my loud, evil days
Calm and unhaunted as is thy dark tent,
Whose peace but by some angel's wing or voice
     Is seldom rent;
   Then I in heaven all the long year
   Would keep, and never wander here.

But living where the sun
Doth all things wake, and where all mix and tire
Themselves and others, I consent and run
     To every mire;
   And by this world's ill-guiding light,
   Err more than I can do by night.

There is in God (some say)
A deep, but dazzling darkness; as men here
Say it is late and dusky, because they
     See not all clear.
   O for that night! where I in him
   Might live invisible and dim.

Henry Vaughan.

THE DAWNING

A H ! what time wilt thou come? when shall that cry
" *The Bridegroom's coming!* " fill the sky?
Shall it in the evening run
When our words and works are done?
Or will thy all-surprising light
     Break at midnight,
When either sleep, or some dark pleasure
Possesseth mad man without measure?
Or shall these early, fragrant hours
     Unlock thy bowers
And with their blush of light descry
Thy locks crowned with eternity?
Indeed, it is the only time
That with thy glory doth best chime;
All now are stirring, ev'ry field
     Full hymns doth yield,

61

The whole Creation shakes off night,
And for thy shadow looks the light;
Stars now vanish without number,
Sleepy planets set and slumber,
The pursy clouds disband and scatter,
All expect some sudden matter;
Not one beam triumphs, but from far
      That morning-star.
Oh at what time soever thou,
Unknown to us, the heavens wilt bow,
And with thy angels in the van,
Descend to judge poor careless man,
Grant I may not like puddle lie
In a corrupt security,
Where, if a traveller water crave,
He finds it dead, and in a grave.
But as this restless, vocal spring
All day and night doth run, and sing,
And though here born, yet is acquainted
Elsewhere, and flowing keeps untainted;
So let me all my busy age
In thy free services engage;
And though (while here) of force I must
Have commerce sometimes with poor dust,
And in my flesh, though vile and low,
As this doth in her channel, flow,
Yet let my course, my aim, my love
And chief acquaintance be above;
So when that day and hour shall come,
In which thyself will be the sun,
Thou'lt find me dress'd and on my way,
Watching the break of thy great day.
            Henry Vaughan.

ANGUISH

M Y God and King! to Thee
    I bow my knee;
I bow my troubled soul, and greet
With my foul heart thy holy feet.
Cast it, or tread it! it shall do
Even what thou wilt, and praise thee too.

My God, could I weep blood,
    Gladly I would,
Or if thou wilt give me that art,
Which through the eyes pours out the heart,
I will exhaust it all, and make
Myself all tears, a weeping lake.

O ! 'tis an easy thing
    To write and sing ;
But to write true, unfeigned verse
Is very hard ! O God, disperse
These weights, and give my spirit leave
To act as well as to conceive !

    O my God, hear my cry ;
      Or let me die ! . . .
                  Henry Vaughan.

PHILLADA FLOUTS ME

O WHAT a plague is love !
    How shall I bear it ?
She will inconstant prove,
    I greatly fear it.
She so torments my mind
    That my strength faileth,
And wavers with the wind
    As a ship saileth.
Please her the best I may,
She loves still to gainsay ;
Alack and well-a-day !
    Phillada flouts me.

At the fair yesterday
    She did pass by me ;
She look'd another way
    And would not spy me :
I woo'd her for to dine,
    But could not get her ;
Will had her to the wine—
    He might entreat her.

63

With Daniel she did dance,
On me she look'd askance :
O thrice unhappy chance !
   Phillada flouts me.

Fair maid, be not so coy,
   Do not disdain me !
I am my mother's joy :
   Sweet, entertain me !
She'll give me, when she dies,
   All that is fitting:
Her poultry and her bees,
   And her goose sitting,
A pair of mattrass beds,
And a bag full of shreds ;
And yet, for all these goods,
   Phillada flouts me !

She hath a clout of mine
   Wrought with blue coventry,
Which she keeps for a sign
   Of my fidelity :
But i' faith, if she flinch
   She shall not wear it ;
To Tib, my t'other wench,
   I mean to bear it.
And yet it grieves my heart
So soon from her to part :
Death strike me with his dart !
   Phillada flouts me.

Thou shalt eat crudded cream
   All the year lasting,
And drink the crystal stream
   Pleasant in tasting ;
Whig and whey whilst thou lust,
   And bramble-berries,
Pie-lid and pastry-crust,
   Pears, plums, and cherries.
Thy raiment shall be thin,
Made of a weevil's skin—

Yet all's not worth a pin !
 Phillada flouts me.

In the last month of May
 I made her posies ;
I heard her often say
 That she loved roses.
Cowslips and gillyflowers
 And the white lily
I brought to deck the bowers
 For my sweet Philly.
But she did all disdain,
And threw them back again ;
Therefore 'tis flat and plain
 Phillada flouts me.

Fair maiden, have a care,
 And in time take me ;
I can have those as fair
 If you forsake me :
For Doll the dairy-maid
 Laugh'd at me lately,
And wanton Winifred
 Favours me greatly.
One throws milk on my clothes,
T'other plays with my nose ;
What wanting signs are those ?
 Phillada flouts me.

I cannot work nor sleep
 At all in season :
Love wounds my heart so deep,
 Without all reason.
I 'gin to pine away
 In my love's shadow,
Like as a fat beast may,
 Penn'd in a meadow.
I shall be dead, I fear,
Within this thousand year :
And all for that my dear
 Phillada flouts me.   *Anonymous.*

D

LOVE'S SECRET

NEVER seek to tell thy love,
    Love that never told can be ;
For the gentle wind does move
    Silently, invisibly.

I told my love, I told my love,
    I told her all my heart ;
Trembling, cold, in ghastly fears,
    Ah ! she did depart !

Soon as she was gone from me,
    A traveller came by,
Silently, invisibly :
    He took her with a sigh.
             William Blake.

MILTON

AND did those feet in ancient time
Walk upon England's mountains green ?
And was the Holy Lamb of God
On England's pleasant pastures seen ?

And did the countenance divine
Shine forth upon our clouded hills ?
And was Jerusalem builded here
Among these dark satanic mills ?

Bring me my bow of burning gold !
Bring me my arrows of desire !
Bring me my spear ! O clouds, unfold !
Bring me my chariot of fire !

I will not cease from mental fight,
Nor shall my sword sleep in my hand,
Till we have built Jerusalem
In England's green and pleasant land.
             William Blake.

66

I WANDERED LONELY

I WANDERED lonely as a cloud
That floats on high o'er vales and hills,
When all at once I saw a crowd,
A host of golden daffodils;
Beside the lake, beneath the trees,
Fluttering and dancing in the breeze.

Continuous as the stars that shine
And twinkle on the milky way,
They stretched in never-ending line
Along the margin of a bay:
Ten thousand saw I at a glance,
Tossing their heads in sprightly dance.

The waves beside them danced; but they
Out-did the sparkling waves in glee.
A poet could not be but gay,
In such a jocund company:
I gazed—and gazed—but little thought
What wealth the show to me had brought:

For oft, when on my couch I lie
In vacant or in pensive mood,
They flash upon that inward eye
Which is the bliss of solitude;
And then my heart with pleasure fills,
And dances with the daffodils.

William Wordsworth.

HUMAN LIFE

IF dead, we cease to be; if total gloom
  Swallow up life's brief flash for ay, we fare
As summer-gusts, of sudden birth and doom,
  Whose sound and motion not alone declare,
But are their whole of being! If the breath
  Be Life itself, and not its task and tent,
If even a soul like Milton's can know death;
  O Man! thou vessel purposeless, unmeant,

Yet drone-hive strange of phantom purposes!
  Surplus of nature's dread activity,
Which, as she gazed on some nigh-finish'd vase,
Retreating slow, with meditative pause,
  She form'd with restless hands unconsciously!
Blank accident! nothing's anomaly!
  If rootless thus, thus substanceless thy state,
Go, weigh thy dreams, and be thy hopes, thy fears,
The counter-weights!—Thy laughter and thy tears
  Mean but themselves, each fittest to create,

And to repay the other! Why rejoices
  Thy heart with hollow joy for hollow good?
  Why cowl thy face beneath the mourner's hood,
Why waste thy sighs, and thy lamenting voices,
  Image of Image, Ghost of Ghostly Elf,
That such a thing as thou feel'st warm or cold?
Yet what and whence thy gain, if thou withhold
  These costless shadows of thy shadowy self?
Be sad! be glad! be neither! seek, or shun!
Thou hast no reason why! Thou canst have none;
Thy being's being is contradiction.

                    S. T. Coleridge.

JENNY KISS'D ME

JENNY kiss'd me when we met,
  Jumping from the chair she sat in;
Time, you thief, who love to get
  Sweets into your list, put that in!
Say I'm weary, say I'm sad,
  Say that health and wealth have miss'd me,
Say I'm growing old, but add,
  Jenny kiss'd me.

                    Leigh Hunt.

WE'LL GO NO MORE A-ROVING

SO, we'll go no more a-roving
  So late into the night,
Though the heart be still as loving,
  And the moon be still as bright.

For the sword outwears its sheath,
　And the soul wears out the breast,
And the heart must pause to breathe,
　And love itself have rest.

Though the night was made for loving,
　And the day returns too soon,
Yet we'll go no more a-roving
　By the light of the moon.
　　　　　　　　　Byron.

LOVE'S PHILOSOPHY

THE fountains mingle with the river
　And the rivers with the ocean,
The winds of heaven mix for ever
　With a sweet emotion;
Nothing in the world is single;
　All things by a law divine
In one another's being mingle.
　Why not I with thine?

See the mountains kiss high heaven
　And the waves clasp one another;
No sister-flower would be forgiven
　If it disdained its brother;
And the sunlight clasps the earth
　And the moonbeams kiss the sea:
What are all these kissings worth
　If thou kiss not me?
　　　　　　　　P. B. Shelley.

TO NIGHT

SWIFTLY walk o'er the western wave,
　Spirit of Night!
Out of the misty eastern cave,
Where, all the long and lone day-light,
Thou wovest dreams of joy and fear,
Which make thee terrible and dear—
　Swift be thy flight!

69

Wrap thy form in a mantle gray,
  Star-inwrought !
Blind with thine hair the eyes of Day ;
Kiss her until she be wearied out,
Then wander o'er city, and sea, and land,
Touching all with thine opiate wand—
  Come, long-sought !

When I arose and saw the dawn,
  I sighed for thee ;
When light rode high, and the dew was gone,
And noon lay heavy on flower and tree,
And the weary day turned to his rest,
Lingering like an unloved guest,
  I sighed for thee.

Thy brother Death came, and cried,
  Wouldst thou me ?
Thy sweet child Sleep, the filmy-eyed,
Murmured like a noontide bee,
Shall I nestle near thy side ?
Wouldst thou me ?—And I replied,
  No, not thee !

Death will come when thou art dead,
  Soon, too soon—
Sleep will come when thou art fled ;
Of neither would I ask the boon
I ask of thee, belovéd Night—
Swift be thine approaching flight,
  Come soon, soon !

                              P. B. Shelley.

WRITTEN IN THE FIELDS

T O one who has been long in city pent,
'Tis very sweet to look into the fair
And open face of heaven,—to breathe a prayer
Full in the smile of the blue firmament.
Who is more happy, when, with heart's content,
Fatigued he sinks into some pleasant lair

70

Of wavy grass, and reads a debonair
And gentle tale of love and languishment ?
Returning home at evening, with an ear
Catching the notes of Philomel,—an eye
Watching the sailing cloudlet's bright career,
He mourns that day so soon has glided by :
E'en like the passage of an angel's tear,
That falls through the clear ether silently.

John Keats.

DAYS

DAUGHTERS of Time, the hypocritic Days,
Muffled and dumb like barefoot dervishes
And marching single in an endless file,
Bring diadems and faggots in their hands.
To each they offer gifts after his will—
Bread, kingdoms, stars, and sky that holds them all.
I, in my pleached garden, watch'd the pomp,
Forgot my morning wishes, hastily
Took a few herbs and apples, and the day
Turn'd and departed silent. I, too late,
Under her solemn fillet saw the scorn.

Ralph Waldo Emerson.

A FAREWELL

FLOW down, cold rivulet, to the sea,
  Thy tribute wave deliver :
No more by thee my steps shall be,
  For ever and for ever.

Flow, softly flow, by lawn and lea,
  A rivulet then a river :
Nowhere by thee my steps shall be,
  For ever and for ever.

But here will sigh thine alder tree,
  And here thine aspen shiver ;
And here by thee will hum the bee,
  For ever and for ever.

71

A thousand suns will stream on thee,
  A thousand moons will quiver;
But not by thee my steps shall be,
  For ever and for ever.   *Tennyson.*

TWO IN THE CAMPAGNA

I WONDER do you feel to-day
  As I have felt since, hand in hand,
We sat down on the grass, to stray
  In spirit better through the land,
This morn of Rome and May?

For me, I touched a thought, I know,
  Has tantalized me many times,
(Like turns of thread the spiders throw
  Mocking across our path) for rhymes
To catch at and let go.

Help me to hold it!   First it left
  The yellowing fennel, run to seed
There, branching from the brickwork's cleft,
  Some old tomb's ruin; yonder weed
Took up the floating weft,

Where one small orange cup amassed
  Five beetles—blind and green they grope
Among the honey-meal; and last,
  Everywhere on the grassy slope
I traced it.   Hold it fast!

The champaign with its endless fleece
  Of feathery grasses everywhere!
Silence and passion, joy and peace,
  An everlasting wash of air—
Rome's ghost since her decease.

Such life here, through such length of hours,
  Such miracles performed in play,
Such primal naked forms of flowers,
  Such letting Nature have her way
While Heaven looks from its towers!

How say you ?   Let us, O my dove,
　　Let us be unashamed of soul,
As earth lies bare to heaven above !
　　How is it under our control
To love or not to love ?

I would that you were all to me,
　　You that are just so much, no more,
Nor yours, nor mine, nor slave nor free !
　　Where does the fault lie ?   What the core
Of the wound, since wound must be ?

I would I could adopt your will,
　　See with your eyes, and set my heart
Beating by yours, and drink my fill
　　At your soul's springs,—your part my part
In life, for good and ill.

No.   I yearn upward, touch you close,
　　Then stand away.   I kiss your cheek,
Catch your soul's warmth—I pluck the rose
　　And love it more than tongue can speak—
Then the good minute goes.

Already how am I so far
　　Out of that minute ?   Must I go
Still like the thistle-ball, no bar,
　　Onward, whenever light winds blow,
Fixed by no friendly star ?

Just when I seemed about to learn !
　　Where is the thread now ?   Off again !
The old trick !   Only I discern—
　　Infinite passion, and the pain
Of finite hearts that yearn.
                                    Robert Browning.

MAGNA EST VERITAS

HERE, in this little Bay,
Full of tumultuous life and great repose,
Where, twice a day,
The purposeless, glad ocean comes and goes,
Under high cliffs, and far from the huge town,
I sit me down.

For want of me the world's course will not fail :
When all its work is done, the lie shall rot ;
The truth is great, and shall prevail,
When none cares whether it prevail or not.

Coventry Patmore.

LIFE OF LIFE

WHAT'S that, which, ere I spake, was gone
So joyful and intense a spark
That, whilst o'erhead the wonder shone,
The day, before but dull, grew dark ?
I do not know ; but this I know,
That, had the splendour lived a year,
The truth that I some heavenly show
Did see, could not be now more clear.
This know I too : might mortal breath
Express the passion then inspired,
Evil would die a natural death,
And nothing transient be desired ;
And error from the soul would pass,
And leave the senses pure and strong
As sunbeams.   But the best, alas,
Has neither memory nor tongue.

Coventry Patmore.

LOVE SIGHT

WHEN do I see thee most, beloved one ?
   When in the light the spirits of mine eyes
   Before thy face, their altar, solemnize
The worship of that Love through thee made known ?
Or when, in the dusk hours, (we two alone,)
   Close-kiss'd and eloquent of still replies
   Thy twilight-hidden glimmering visage lies,
And my soul only sees thy soul its own ?

O love, my love ! if I no more should see
Thyself, nor on the earth the shadow of thee,
   Nor image of thine eyes in any spring,—
How then should sound upon Life's darkening slope
The ground-whirl of the perish'd leaves of Hope,
   The wind of Death's imperishable wing ?

Dante Gabriel Rossetti.

74

THE WOODSPURGE

THE wind flapped loose, the wind was still,
Shaken out dead from tree and hill :
I had walk'd on at the wind's will,—
I sat now, for the wind was still.

Between my knees my forehead was,—
My lips, drawn in, said not Alas !
My hair was over in the grass,
My naked ears heard the day pass.

My eyes, wide open, had the run
Of some ten weeds to fix upon ;
Among those few, out of the sun,
The woodspurge flowered, three cups in one.

From perfect grief there need not be
Wisdom or even memory :
One thing then learnt remains to me,—
The woodspurge has a cup of three.

Dante Gabriel Rossetti.

MODERN LOVE
XLVII

WE saw the swallows gathering in the sky,
And in the osier-isle we heard them noise.
We had not to look back on summer joys,
Or forward to a summer of bright dye :
But in the largeness of the evening earth
Our spirits grew as we went side by side.
The hour became her husband and my bride.
Love that had robbed us so, thus blessed our dearth !
The pilgrims of the year waxed very loud
In multitudinous chatterings, as the flood
Full brown came from the West, and like pale blood
Expanded to the upper crimson cloud.
Love that had robbed us of immortal things,
This little moment mercifully gave,
Where I have seen across the twilight wave
The swan sail with her young beneath her wings.

George Meredith.

SEED-TIME

F L O W E R S of the willow-herb are wool ;
Flowers of the briar berries red ;
Speeding their seed as the breeze may rule.
Flowers of the thistle loosen the thread.
Flowers of the clematis drip in beard,
Slack from the fir-tree youngly climbed ;
Chaplets in air, flies foliage seared ;
Heeled upon earth, lie clusters rimed.

Where were skies of the mantle stained
Orange and scarlet, a coat of frieze
Travels from North till day has waned,
Tattered, soaked in the ditch's dyes ;
Tumbles the rook under grey or slate ;
Else enfolding us, damps to the bone ;
Narrows the world to my neighbour's gate ;
Paints me Life as a wheezy crone.

Now seems none but the spider lord ;
Star in circle his web waits prey,
Silvering bush-mounds, blue brushing sward ;
Slow runs the hour, swift flits the ray.
Now to his thread-shroud is he nigh,
Nigh to the tangle where wings are sealed,
He who frolicked the jewelled fly ;
All is adroop on the down and the weald.

Mists more lone for the sheep-bell enwrap
Nights that tardily let slip a morn
Paler than moons, and on noontide's lap
Flame dies cold, like the rose late born.
Rose born late, born withered in bud !—
I, even I, for a zenith of sun
Cry, to fulfil me, nourish my blood :
O for a day of the long light, one !

Master the blood, nor read by chills,
Earth admonishes : Hast thou ploughed,
Sown, reaped, harvested grain for the mills,
Thou hast the light over shadow of cloud.

Steadily eyeing, before that wail
Animal-infant, thy mind began,
Momently nearer me : should sight fail,
Plod in the track of the husbandman.

Verily now is our season of seed,
Now in our Autumn ; and Earth discerns
Them that have served her in them that can read,
Glassing, where under the surface she burns,
Quick at her wheel, while the fuel, decay,
Brightens the fire of renewal : and we ?
Death is the word of a bovine-day,
Know you the breast of the springing To-be.

George Meredith.

MIRAGE

THE hope I dreamed of was a dream,
  Was but a dream ; and now I wake,
Exceeding comfortless, and worn, and old,
  For a dream's sake.

I hang my harp upon a tree,
  A weeping willow in a lake ;
I hang my silent harp there, wrung and snapt
  For a dream's sake.

Lie still, lie still, my breaking heart ;
  My silent heart, lie still and break :
Life, and the world, and mine own self, are changed
  For a dream's sake.

Christina Rossetti.

WEATHERS

THIS is the weather the cuckoo likes,
    And so do I ;
When showers betumble the chestnut spikes,
    And nestlings fly ;
And the little brown nightingale bills his best,
And they sit outside the " Traveller's Rest,"
And maids come forth sprig-muslin drest,
And citizens dream of the South and West,
    And so do I.

77

This is the weather the shepherd shuns,
    And so do I :
When beeches drip in browns and duns,
    And thresh, and ply ;
And hill-hid tides throb, throe on throe,
And meadow rivulets overflow,
And drops on gate-bars hang in a row,
And rooks in families homeward go,
    And so do I.

Thomas Hardy.

I BENDED UNTO ME

I BENDED unto me a bough of May,
That I might see and smell :
It bore it in a sort of way,
It bore it very well.
But when I let it backward sway,
Then it were hard to tell
With what a toss, with what a swing,
The dainty thing
Resumed its proper level,
And sent me to the devil.
I know it did—you doubt it ?
I turned, and saw them whispering about it.

T. E. Brown.

THE LADY POVERTY

THE Lady Poverty was fair :
But she has lost her looks of late,
With change of times and change of air.
Ah slattern ! she neglects her hair,
Her gown, her shoes ; she keeps no state
As once when her pure feet were bare.

Or—almost worse, if worse can be—
She scolds in parlours, dusts and trims,
Watches and counts.   O is this she
Whom Francis met, whose step was free,
Who with Obedience carolled hymns,
In Umbria walked with Chastity ?

Where is her ladyhood ? Not here,
Not among modern kinds of men ;
But in the stony fields, where clear
Through the thin trees the skies appear,
In delicate spare soil and fen,
And slender landscape and austere.

Alice Meynell.

TO SILENCE

"Space, the bound of a solid " : silence, then, the form of a melody.

NOT, Silence, for thine idleness I raise
My silence-bounded singing in thy praise,
But for thy moulding of my Mozart's tune
Thy hold upon the bird that sings the moon,
      Thy magisterial ways.

Man's lovely definite melody-shapes are thine,
Outlined, controlled, compressed, complete, divine ;
Also thy fine intrusions do I trace,
Thy afterthoughts, thy wandering, thy grace,
      Within the poet's line.

Thy secret is the song that is to be.
Music had never stature but for thee,
Sculptor ! strong as the sculptor Space whose hand
Urged the Discobolus and bade him stand.

Man, on his way to Silence, stops to hear and see.

Alice Meynell.

THE WIND IS BLIND

"Eyeless, in Gaza, at the mill, with slaves."
Milton's *Samson.*

THE wind is blind.
The earth sees sun and moon ; the height
Is watch-tower to the dawn ; the plain
Shines to the summer ; visible light
Is scattered in the drops of rain.

79

The wind is blind.
The flashing billows are aware;
With open eyes the cities see;
Light leaves the ether, everywhere
Known to the homing bird and bee.

The wind is blind,
Is blind alone. How has he hurled
His ignorant lash, his aimless dart,
His eyeless rush upon the world,
Unseeing, to break his unknown heart!

The wind is blind.
And the sail traps him, and the mill
Captures him; and he cannot save
His swiftness and his desperate will
From those blind uses of the slave.

Alice Meynell.

JULY FUGITIVE

CAN you tell me where has hid her
 Pretty Maid July?
I would swear one day ago
 She passed by,
I would swear that I do know
 The blue bliss of her eye:
" Tarry, maid, maid," I bid her;
 But she hastened by.
Do you know where she has hid her,
 Maid July?

Yet in truth it needs must be
 The flight of her is old;
Yet in truth it needs must be,
 For her nest, the earth, is cold.
No more in the poolèd Even
 Wade her rosy feet,
Dawn-flakes no more plash from them
 To poppies 'mid the wheat.

She has muddied the day's oozes
   With her petulant feet;
Scared the clouds that floated,
   As sea-birds they were,
Slow on the coerule
   Lulls of the air,
Lulled on the luminous
   Levels of air:
She has chidden in a pet
   All her stars from her;
Now they wander loose and sigh
   Through the turbid blue,
Now they wander, weep, and cry—
   Yea, and I too—
" Where are you, sweet July,
   Where are you ? "

Who hath beheld her footprints,
   Or the pathway she goes ?
Tell me, wind, tell me, wheat,
   Which of you knows ?
Sleeps she swathed in the flushed Arctic
   Night of the Rose ?
Or lie her limbs like Alp-glow
   On the lily's snows ?
Gales, that are all-visitant,
   Find the runaway;
And for him who findeth her
   (I do charge you say)
I will throw largesse of broom
   Of this summer's mintage,
I will broach a honey-bag
   Of the bee's best vintage.

Breezes, wheat, flowers sweet,
   None of them knows !
How then shall we lure her back
   From the way she goes ?
For it were a shameful thing,
   Saw we not this comer
Ere Autumn camp upon the fields
   Red with rout of Summer.

When the bird quits the cage,
  We set the cage outside,
With seed and with water,
  And the door wide,
Haply we may win it so
  Back to abide.
Hang her cage of Earth out
  O'er Heaven's sunward wall,
Its four gates open, winds in watch
  By reinéd cars at all ;
Relume in hanging hedgerows
  The rain-quenched blossom,
And roses sob their tears out
  On the gale's warm heaving bosom ;
Shake the lilies till their scent
  Over-drip their rims
That our runaway may see
  We do know her whims ;
Sleek the tumbled waters out
  For her travelled limbs ;
Strew and smooth blue night thereon :
  There will—O not doubt her !—
The lovely sleepy lady lie,
  With all her stars about her !

Francis Thompson.

FROM THE NIGHT OF FOREBEING

"In the chaos of preordination, and night of our forebeings."
Sir Thomas Moore.

" Et lux in tenebris erat, et tenebræ eam non comprehenderunt."
St. John.

CAST wide the folding doorways of the East,
For now is light increased !
And the wind-besomed chambers of the air,
See they be garnished fair ;
And look the ways exhale some precious odours,
And set ye all about wild-breathing spice,
Most fit for Paradise !
Now is no time for sober gravity,
Season enough has Nature to be wise ;
But now discint, with raiment glittering free,

Shake she the ringing rafters of the skies
With festal footing and bold joyance sweet,
And let the earth be drunken and carouse!
For lo, into her house
Spring is come home with her world-wandering feet,
And all things are made young with young desires ;
And all for her is light increased
In yellow stars and yellow daffodils,
And East to West, and West to East,
Fling answering welcome-fires,
By dawn and day-fall, on the jocund hills.
And ye, winged minstrels of her fair meinie,
Being newly coated in glad livery,
Upon her steps attend,
And round her treading dance, and without end
Reel your shrill lutany.
What popular breath her coming does out-tell
The garrulous leaves among !
What little noises stir and pass
From blade to blade along the voluble grass !
O Nature, never-done
Ungaped-at Pentecostal miracle,
We hear thee, each man in his proper tongue !
Break, elemental children, break ye loose
From the strict frosty rule
Of grey-beard Winter's school.
Vault, O young winds, vault in your tricksome courses
Upon the snowy steeds that reinless use
In cœrule pampas of the heaven to run ;
Foaled of the white sea-horses,
Washed in the lambent waters of the sun.
Let even the slug-abed snail upon the thorn
Put forth a conscious horn !
Mine elemental co-mates, joy each one ;
And ah, my foster-brethren, seem not sad—
No, seem not sad,
That my strange heart and I should be so little glad.
Suffer me at your leafy feast
To sit apart, a somewhat alien guest,
And watch your mirth,
Unsharing in the liberal laugh of earth ;

Yet with a sympathy
Begot of wholly sad and half-sweet memory—
The little sweetness making grief complete ;
Faint wind of wings from hours that distant beat,
When I, I too,
Was once, O wild companions, as are you,—
Ran with such wilful feet ;
Wraith of a recent day and dead,
Risen wanly overhead,
Frail, strengthless as a noon-belated moon,
Or as the glazing eyes of watery heaven,
When the sick night sinks into deathly swoon.

A higher and a solemn voice
I heard through your gay-hearted noise ;
A solemn meaning and a stiller voice
Sounds to me from far days when I too shall rejoice,
Nor more be with your jollity at strife.
O prophecy
Of things that are, and are not, and shall be !
The great-vanned Angel March
Hath trumpeted
His clangorous " Sleep no more " to all the dead—
Beat his strong vans o'er earth, and air, and sea.
And they have heard ;
Hark to the *Jubilate* of the bird
For them that found the dying way to life !
And they have heard,
And quicken to the great precursive word ;
Green spray showers lightly down the cascade of the larch ;
The graves are riven,
And the Sun comes with power amid the clouds of heaven !
Before his way
Went forth the trumpet of the March ;
Before his way, before his way
Dances the pennon of the May !
O Earth, unchilded, widowed Earth, so long
Lifting in patient pine and ivy-tree
Mournful belief and steadfast prophecy,
Behold now all things are made true !

Behold your bridegroom cometh in to you,
Exceeding glad and strong.
Raise up your eyes, O raise your eyes abroad !
No more shall you sit sole and vidual,
Searching, in servile pall,
Upon the hieratic night the star-sealed sense of all :
Rejoice, O barren, and look forth abroad !
Your children gathered back to your embrace
See with a mother's face.
Look up, O mortals, and the portent heed ;
In very deed,
Washed with new fire to their irradiant birth,
Reintegrated are the heavens and earth !
From sky to sod,
The world's unfolded blossom smells of God.

O imagery
Of that which was the first, and is the last !
For, as the dark profound nativity,
God saw the end should be,
When the world's infant horoscope He cast.
Unshackled from the bright Phœbean awe,
In leaf, flower, mold, and tree,
Resolved into dividual liberty,
Most strengthless, unparticipant, inane,
Or suffered the ill peace of lethargy,
Lo, the Earth eased of rule :
Unsummered, granted to her own worst smart
The dear wish of the fool—
Disintegration, merely which man's heart
For freedom understands,
Amid the frog-like errors from the damp
And quaking swamp
Of the low popular levels spawned in all the lands.
But thou, O Earth, dost much disdain
The bondage of thy waste and futile reign,
And sweetly to the great compulsion draw
Of God's alone true-manumitting law,
And Freedom, only which the wise intend,
To work thine innate end.

85

Over thy vacant counterfeit of death
Broods with soft urgent breath
Love, that is child of Beauty and of Awe :
To intercleavage of sharp warring pain,
As of contending chaos come again,
Thou wak'st, O Earth,
And work'st from change to change and birth to birth
Creation old as hope, and new as sight ;
For meed of toil not vain,
Hearing once more the primal fiat toll :
" Let there be light ! "
And there is light !
Light flagrant, manifest ;
Light to the zenith, light from pole to pole ;
Light from the East that waxeth to the West,
And with its puissant goings-forth
Encroaches on the South and on the North ;
And with its great approaches does prevail
Upon the sullen fastness of the height,
And summoning its levied power
Crescent and confident through the crescent hour,
Goes down with laughters on the subject vale.
Light flagrant, manifest ;
Light to the sentient closeness of the breast,
Light to the secret chambers of the brain !
And thou up-floatest, warm, and newly-bathed,
Earth, through delicious air,
And with thine own apparent beauties swathed,
Wringing the waters from thine arborous hair ;
That all men's hearts, which do behold and see,
Grow weak with their exceeding much desire,
And turn to thee on fire,
Enamoured with their utter wish of thee,
Anadyomene !
What vine-outquickening life all creatures sup,
Feel, for the air within its sapphire cup
How it does leap, and twinkle headily !
Feel, for Earth's bosom pants, and heaves her scarfing
  sea;
And round and round in bacchanal rout reel the swift
  spheres intemperably !

My little-worlded self! the shadows pass
In this thy sister-world, as in a glass,
Of all processions that revolve in thee :
Not only of cyclic Man
Thou here discern'st the plan,
Not only of cyclic Man, but of the cyclic Me.
Not solely of Mortality's great years
The reflex just appears,
But thine own bosom's year, still circling round
In ample and in ampler gyre
Toward the far completion, wherewith crowned,
Love unconsumed shall chant in his own furnace-fire.
How many trampled and deciduous joys
Enrich thy soul for joys deciduous still,
Before the distance shall fulfil
Cyclic unrest with solemn equipoise !
Happiness is the shadow of things past,
Which fools still take for that which is to be !
And not all foolishly :
For all the past, read true, is prophecy,
And all the firsts are hauntings of some Last,
And all the springs are flash-lights of one Spring,
Then leaf, and flower, and fall-less fruit
Shall hang together on the unyellowing bough ;
And silence shall be Music mute
For her surchargéd heart.   Hush thou !
These things are far too sure that thou should'st dream
Thereof, lest they appear as things that seem.

Shade within shade ! for deeper in the glass
Now other imaged meanings pass ;
And as the man, the poet there is read.
Winter with me, alack !
Winter on every hand I find :
Soul, brain, and pulses dead,
The mind no further by the warm sense fed,
The soul weak-stirring in the arid mind,
More tearless-weak to flash itself abroad
Than the earth's life beneath the frost-scorched sod.
My lips have drought, and crack,
By laving music long unvisited.

Beneath the austere and macerating rime
Draws back constricted in its icy urns
The genial flame of Earth, and there
With torment and with tension does prepare
The lush disclosures of the vernal time.
All joys draw inward to their icy urns,
Tormented by constraining rime,
And there,
With undelight and throe prepare
The bounteous efflux of the vernal time.
Nor less beneath compulsive Law
Rebukéd draw
The numbéd musics back upon my heart ;
Whose yet-triumphant course I know
And prevalent pulses forth shall start,
    Like cataracts that with thunderous hoof charge the
      disbanding snow.
All power is bound
In quickening refusal so ;
And silence is the lair of sound ;
In act its impulse to deliver,
With fluctuance and quiver
The endeavouring thew grows rigid.   Strong
From its retracted coil strikes the resilient song.

Giver of spring,
And song, and every young new thing !
Thou only seest in me, so stripped and bare,
The lyric secret waiting to be born,
The patient term allowed
Before it stretch and flutteringly unfold
Its rumpled webs of amethyst-freaked, diaphanous gold.
And what hard task abstracts me from delight,
Filling with hopeless hope and dear despair
The still-born day and parchéd fields of night,
That my old way of song, no longer fair,
For lack of serene care,
Is grown a stony and a weed-choked plot,
Thou only know'st aright,
Thou only know'st, for I know not.

88

How many songs must die that this may live !
And shall this most rash hope and fugitive,
Fulfilled with beauty and with might
In days whose feet are rumorous on the air,
Make me forget to grieve
For songs which might have been, nor ever were ?
Stern the denial, the travail slow,
The struggling wall will scantly grow :
And though with that dread rite of sacrifice
Ordained for during edifice,
How long, how long ago !
Into that wall which will not thrive
I build myself alive,
Ah, who shall tell me will the wall uprise ?
Thou wilt not tell me, who dost only know !
Yet still in mind I keep,
He that observes the wind shall hardly sow,
He that regards the clouds shall hardly reap.
Thine ancient way !   I give,
Nor wit if I receive ;
Risk all, who all would gain : and blindly.   Be it so.

" And blindly," said I ?—No !
That saying I unsay : the wings
Hear I not in prævenient winnowings
Of coming songs, that lift my hair and stir it ?
What winds with music wet do the sweet storm foreshow !
Utter stagnation
Is the solstitial slumber of the spirit,
The blear and blank negation of all life :
But these sharp questionings mean strife, and strife
Is the negation of negation.
The thing from which I turn my troubled look,
Fearing the gods' rebuke ;
That perturbation putting glory on,
As is the golden vortex in the West
Over the foundered sun ;
That—but low breathe it, lest the Nemesis
Unchild me, vaunting this—
Is bliss, the hid, hugged, swaddled bliss !
O youngling Joy carest !

That on my now first-mothered breast
Pliest the strange wonder of thine infant lip
What this aghast surprise of keenest panging,
Wherefrom I blench, and cry thy soft mouth rest ?
Ah hold, withhold, and let the sweet mouth slip !
So, with such pain, recoils the woolly dam,
Unused, affrighted, from her yeanling lamb :
I, one with her in cruel fellowship,
Marvel what unmaternal thing I am.

Nature, enough ! Within thy glass
Too many and too stern the shadows pass.
In this delighted season, flaming
For thy resurrection-feast,
Ah, more I think the long ensepulture cold,
Than stony winter rolled
From the unsealed mouth of the holy East ;
The snowdrop's saintly stoles less heed
Than the snow-cloistered penance of the seed.
'Tis the weak flesh reclaiming
Against the ordinance
Which yet for just the accepting spirit scans.
Earth waits, and patient heaven,
Self-bonded God doth wait
Thrice-promulgated bans
Of His fair nuptial-date.
And power is man's,
With that great word of " Wait,"
To still the sea of tears,
And shake the iron heart of Fate.
In that one word is strong
An else, alas, much-mortal song ;
With sight to pass the frontier of all spheres,
And voice which does my sight such wrong.

Not without fortitude I wait
The dark majestical ensuit
Of destiny, nor peevish rate
Calm-knowledged Fate.
I, that no part have in the time's bragged way,
And its loud bruit ;

I, in this house so rifted, marred,
So ill to live in, hard to leave ;
I, so star-weary, over-warred,
That have no joy in this your day—
Rather foul fume englutting, that of day
Confounds all ray—
But only stand aside and grieve ;
I yet have sight beyond the smoke,
And kiss the gods' feet, though they wreak
Upon me stroke and again stroke ;
And this my seeing is not weak.
The Woman I behold, whose vision seek
All eyes and know not ; t'ward whom climb
The steps o' the world, and beats all wing of rhyme,
And knows not ; 'twixt the sun and moon
Her inexpressible front enstarred
Tempers the wrangling spheres to tune ;
Their divergent harmonies
Concluded in the concord of her eyes,
And vestal dances of her glad regard.
I see, which fretteth with surmise
Much heads grown unsagacious-grey,
The slow aim of wise-hearted Time,
Which folded cycles within cycles cloak ;
We pass, we pass, we pass ; this does not pass away,
But holds the furrowing earth still harnessed to its yoke.
The stars still write their golden purposes
On heaven's high palimpsest, and no man sees,
Nor any therein Daniel ; I do hear
From the revolving year
A voice which cries :
" All dies ;
Lo, how all dies ! O seer,
And all things too arise :
All dies, and all is born ;   [Morn."
But each resurgent morn, behold, more near the Perfect

Firm is the man, and set beyond the cast
Of Fortune's game, and the iniquitous hour,
Whose falcon soul sits fast,
And not intends her high sagacious tour

Or ere the quarry sighted ; who looks past
To slow much sweet from little instant sour,
And in the first does always see the last.

Francis Thompson.

MY BODY WHICH MY DUNGEON IS

M Y body, which my dungeon is,
And yet my parks and palaces :—
   Which is so great that there I go
All the day long to and fro,
And when the night begins to fall
Throw down my bed and sleep, while all
The building hums with wakefulness—
Even as a child of savages
When evening takes her on her way,
(She having roamed a summer's day
Along the mountain-sides and scalp)
Sleeps in the antre of that alp :—
   Which is so broad and high that there,
As in the topless field of air,
My fancy soars like to a kite
And faints in the blue infinite :—
   Which is so strong, my strongest throes
And the rough world's besieging blows
Not break it, and so weak withal,
Death ebbs and flows in its loose wall
As the green sea in fishers' nets,
And tops its topmost parapets :—
   Which is so wholly mine that I
Can wield its whole artillery,
And mine so little, that my soul
Dwells in perpetual control,
And I but think and speak and do
As my dead fathers move me to :—
   If this born body of my bones
The beggared soul so barely owns,
What money passed from hand to hand,
What creeping custom of the land,
What deed of author or assign,
Can make a house a thing of mine ?

R. L. Stevenson.

SLOW SPRING

O YEAR, grow slowly. Exquisite, holy,
   The days go on
With almonds showing the pink stars blowing,
   And birds in the dawn.

Grow slowly, year, like a child that is dear,
   Or a lamb that is mild,
By little steps, and by little skips,
   Like a lamb or a child.

                              Katharine Tynan.

THAT THE NIGHT COME

SHE lived in storm and strife,
Her soul had such desire
For what proud death may bring
That it could not endure
The common good of life,
But lived as 'twere a king
That packed his marriage day
With banneret and pennon,
Trumpet and kettledrum,
And the outrageous cannon,
To bundle time away
That the night come.

                              W. B. Yeats.

SOLOMON AND THE WITCH

AND thus declared that Arab lady :
" Last night, where under the wild moon
On grassy mattress I had laid me,
Within my arms great Solomon,
I suddenly cried out in a strange tongue
Not his, not mine."
                    And he that knew
All sounds by bird or angel sung
Answered : " A crested cockerel crew
Upon a blossoming apple bough
Three hundred years before the Fall,
And never crew again till now,

93

And would not now but that he thought,
Chance being at one with Choice at last,
All that the brigand apple brought
And this foul world were dead at last.
He that crowed out eternity
Thought to have crowed it in again.
A lover with a spider's eye
Will find out some appropriate pain,
Aye, though all passion's in the glance,
For every nerve : lover tests lover
With cruelties of Choice and Chance ;
And when at last that murder's over
Maybe the bride-bed brings despair,
For each an imagined image brings
And finds a real image there ;
Yet the world ends when these two things,
Though several, are a single light,
When oil and wick are burned in one ;
Therefore a blessed moon last night
Gave Sheba to her Solomon."

" Yet the world stays " :

                              " If that be so,
Your cockerel found us in the wrong
Although he thought it worth a crow.
Maybe an image is too strong
Or maybe is not strong enough."

" The night has fallen ; not a sound
In the forbidden sacred grove,
Unless a petal hit the ground,
Nor any human sight within it
But the crushed grass where we have lain ;
And the moon is wilder every minute.
Oh, Solomon ! let us try again."

                                        W. B. Yeats.

IN THE POPPY FIELD

MAD Patsy said, he said to me,
That every morning he could see
An angel walking on the sky;
Across the sunny skies of morn
He threw great handfuls far and nigh
Of poppy seed among the corn;
And then, he said, the angels run
To see the poppies in the sun.

A poppy is a devil weed,
I said to him—he disagreed;
He said the devil had no hand
In spreading flowers tall and fair
Through corn and rye and meadow land,
By garth and barrow everywhere:
The devil has not any flower,
But only money in his power.

And then he stretched out in the sun
And rolled upon his back for fun:
He kicked his legs and roared for joy
Because the sun was shining down,
He said he was a little boy
And would not work for any clown:
He ran and laughed behind a bee,
And danced for very ecstasy.

James Stephens.

THE SNARE

I HEAR a sudden cry of pain!
  There is a rabbit in a snare:
Now I hear the cry again,
  But I cannot tell from where.

But I cannot tell from where
  He is calling out for aid;
Crying on the frightened air,
  Making everything afraid.

95

Making everything afraid,
  Wrinkling up his little face,
As he cries again for aid;
  And I cannot find the place!

And I cannot find the place
  Where his paw is in the snare:
Little one! Oh, little one!
  I am searching everywhere!

James Stephens

LEISURE

W H A T is this life if, full of care,
We have no time to stand and stare.

No time to stand beneath the boughs
And stare as long as sheep or cows.

No time to see, when woods we pass,
Where squirrels hide their nuts in grass.

No time to see, in broad daylight,
Streams full of stars, like stars at night.

No time to turn at Beauty's glance,
And watch her feet, how they can dance.

No time to wait till her mouth can
Enrich that smile her eyes began.

A poor life this if, full of care,
We have no time to stand and stare.

W. H. Davies.

THE LIKENESS

W H E N I came forth this morn I saw
  Quite twenty cloudlets in the air;
And then I saw a flock of sheep,
  Which told me how those clouds came there.

96

That flock of sheep, on that green grass,
  Well might it lie so still and proud !
Its likeness had been drawn in heaven,
  On a blue sky, in silvery cloud.

I gazed me up, I gazed me down,
  And swore, though good the likeness was,
'Twas a long way from justice done
  To such white wool, such sparkling grass.

                              W. H. Davies.

THE TWO CHILDREN

"AH, little boy ! I see
  You have a wooden spade.
Into this sand you dig
  So deep—for what ? " I said.
" There's more rich gold," said he,
  " Down under where I stand,
Than twenty elephants
  Could move across the land."

" Ah, little girl with wool !—
  What are you making now ? "
" Some stockings for a bird,
  To keep his legs from snow."
And there those children are,
  So happy, small, and proud :
The boy that digs his grave,
  The girl that knits her shroud.

                              W. H. Davies.

A GREAT TIME

SWEET Chance, that led my steps abroad,
  Beyond the town, where wild flowers grow—
A rainbow and a cuckoo, Lord,
  How rich and great the times are now !
    Know, all ye sheep
    And cows, that keep

On staring that I stand so long
  In grass that's wet from heavy rain—
A rainbow and a cuckoo's song
  May never come together again ;
    May never come
    This side the tomb.
                W. H. Davies.

THE BELLS OF HEAVEN

'T W O U L D ring the bells of Heaven
The wildest peal for years,
If Parson lost his senses
And people came to theirs,
And he and they together
Knelt down with angry prayers
For tamed and shabby tigers
And dancing dogs and bears,
And wretched, blind pit ponies,
And little hunted hares.
                Ralph Hodgson.

TIME, YOU OLD GIPSY MAN

T I M E , you old gipsy man,
  Will you not stay,
Put up your caravan
  Just for one day ?

All things I'll give you
Will you be my guest,
Bells for your jennet
Of silver the best,
Goldsmiths shall beat you
A great golden ring,
Peacocks shall bow to you,
Little boys sing,
Oh, and sweet girls will
Festoon you with may,
Time, you old gipsy,
Why hasten away ?

Last week in Babylon,
Last night in Rome,
Morning, and in the crush
Under Paul's dome ;
Under Paul's dial
You tighten your rein—
Only a moment,
And off once again ;
Off to some city
Now blind in the womb,
Off to another
Ere that's in the tomb.

Time, you old gipsy man,
   Will you not stay,
Put up your caravan
   Just for one day ?

Ralph Hodgson.

BY A BIER-SIDE

THIS is a sacred city built of marvellous earth.
Life was lived nobly here to give such beauty birth.
Beauty was in this brain and in this eager hand :
Death is so blind and dumb Death does not understand.
Death drifts the brain with dust and soils the young limbs'
   glory,
Death makes justice a dream, and strength a traveller's
   story.
Death drives the lovely soul to wander under the sky,
Death opens unknown doors.   It is most grand to die.

John Masefield.

INVOCATION

O WANDERER into many brains
O spark the emperor's purple hides,
You sow the dusk with fiery grains
When the gold horseman rides.
   O beauty on the darkness hurled,
   Be it through me you shame the world.

John Masefield.

99

TO HIS MOTHER, C.L.M.

I N the dark womb where I began
My mother's life made me a man.
Through all the months of human birth
Her beauty fed my common earth.
I cannot see, nor breathe, nor stir,
But through the death of some of her.

Down in the darkness of the grave
She cannot see the life she gave.
For all her love, she cannot tell
Whether I use it ill or well,
Nor knock at dusty doors to find
Her beauty dusty in the mind.

If the grave's gates could be undone,
She would not know her little son,
I am so grown.   If we should meet,
She would pass by me in the street,
Unless my soul's face let her see
My sense of what she did for me.

What have I done to keep in mind
My debt to her and womankind ?
What woman's happier life repays
Her for those months of wretched days ?
For all my mouthless body leech'd
Ere Birth's releasing hell was reach'd ?

What have I done, or tried, or said
In thanks to that dear woman dead ?
Men triumph over women still,
Men trample women's rights at will,
And man's lust roves the world untamed.

.   .   .   .   .

O grave, keep shut lest I be shamed.

John Masefield.

ECCLESIASTES

THERE is one sin : to call a green leaf grey,
  Whereat the sun in heaven shuddereth.
There is one blasphemy : for death to pray,
  For God alone knoweth the praise of death.

There is one creed : 'neath no world-terror's wing
  Apples forget to grow on apple-trees.
There is one thing is needful—everything—
  The rest is vanity of vanities.

G. K. Chesterton.

THE PRAISE OF DUST

" WHAT of vile dust ? " the preacher said.
  Methought the whole world woke,
The dead stone lived beneath my foot,
  And my whole body spoke.

" You, that play tyrant to the dust,
  And stamp its wrinkled face,
This patient star that flings you not
  Far into homeless space,

" Come down out of your dusty shrine
  The living dust to see,
The flowers that at your sermon's end
  Stand blazing silently.

" Rich white and blood-red blossom ; stones,
  Lichens like fire encrust ;
A gleam of blue, a glare of gold,
  The vision of the dust.

" Pass them all by : till, as you come
  Where, at a city's edge,
Under a tree—I know it well—
  Under a lattice ledge,

" The sunshine falls on one brown head.
  You, too, O cold of clay,
Eater of stones, may haply hear
  The trumpets of that day

" When God to all his paladins
By his own splendour swore
To make a fairer face than heaven,
Of dust and nothing more."

G. K. Chesterton.

WINE AND WATER

O L D Noah he had an ostrich farm and fowls on the largest scale,
He ate his egg with a ladle in an egg-cup big as a pail,
And the soup he took was Elephant Soup, and the fish he took was Whale,
But they all were small to the cellar he took when he set out to sail,
And Noah he often said to his wife when he sat down to dine,
" I don't care where the water goes if it doesn't get into the wine."

The cataract of the cliff of heaven fell blinding off the brink
As if it would wash the stars away as suds go down a sink,
The seven heavens came roaring down for the throats of hell to drink,
And Noah he cocked his eye and said, " It looks like rain, I think,
The water has drowned the Matterhorn as deep as a Mendip mine,
But I don't care where the water goes if it doesn't get into the wine."

But Noah he sinned, and we have sinned ; on tipsy feet we trod,
Till a great big black teetotaller was sent to us for a rod,
And you can't get wine at a P.S.A., or chapel, or Eisteddfod.
For the Curse of Water has come again because of the wrath of God,
And water is on the Bishop's board and the Higher Thinker's shrine,
But I don't care where the water goes if it doesn't get into the wine.

G. K. Chesterton.

MENDING WALL

SOMETHING there is that doesn't love a wall,
That sends the frozen-ground-swell under it,
And spills the upper boulders in the sun;
And makes gaps even two can pass abreast.
The work of hunters is another thing:
I have come after them and made repair
Where they have left not one stone on stone,
But they would have the rabbit out of hiding,
To please the yelping dogs.   The gaps I mean,
No one has seen them made or heard them made,
But at spring mending-time we find them there.
I let my neighbour know beyond the hill;
And on a day we meet to walk the line
And set the wall between us once again.
We keep the wall between us as we go.
To each the boulders that have fallen to each.
And some are loaves and some so nearly balls
We have to use a spell to make them balance:
"Stay where you are until our backs are turned!"
We wear our fingers rough with handling them.
Oh, just another kind of out-door game,
One on a side.   It comes to little more:
There where it is we do not need the wall:
He is all pine and I am apple orchard.
My apple trees will never get across
And eat the cones under his pines, I tell him.
He only says, " Good fences make good neighbours."
Spring is the mischief in me, and I wonder
If I could put a notion in his head:
" Why do they make good neighbours?   Isn't it
Where there are cows?   But here there are no cows.
Before I built a wall I'd ask to know
What I was walling in or walling out,
And to whom I was like to give offence.
Something there is that doesn't love a wall,
That wants it down."   I could say " Elves " to him,
But it's not elves exactly, and I'd rather
He said it for himself.   I see him there
Bringing a stone grasped firmly by the top

In each hand, like an old-stone savage armed.
He moves in darkness as it seems to me,
Not of woods only and the shade of trees.
He will not go behind his father's saying,
And he likes having thought of it so well
He says again, " Good fences make good neighbours."

Robert Frost.

TO A POET A THOUSAND YEARS HENCE

I WHO am dead a thousand years,
   And wrote this sweet archaic song,
Send you my words for messengers
   The way I shall not pass along.

I care not if you bridge the seas,
   Or ride secure the cruel sky,
Or build consummate palaces
   Of metal or of masonry.

But have you wine and music still,
   And statues and a bright-eyed love,
And foolish thoughts of good or ill,
   And prayers to them who sit above?

How shall we conquer? Like a wind
   That falls at eve our fancies blow,
And old Mæonides the blind
   Said it three thousand years ago.

O friend unseen, unborn, unknown,
   Student of our sweet English tongue,
Read out my words at night, alone,
   I was a poet, I was young.

Since I can never see your face,
   And never shake you by the hand,
I send my soul through time and space
   To greet you. You will understand.

James Elroy Flecker.

THE BALLAD OF HAMPSTEAD HEATH

FROM Heaven's Gate to Hampstead Heath
   Young Bacchus and his crew
Came tumbling down, and o'er the town
   Their bursting trumpets blew.

The silver night was wildly bright,
   And madly shone the Moon
To hear a song so clear and strong,
   With such a lovely tune.

From London's houses, huts and flats,
   Came busmen, snobs, and Earls,
And ugly men in bowler hats
   With charming little girls.

Sir Moses came with eyes of flame,
   Judd, who is like a bloater,
The brave Lord Mayor in coach and pair,
   King Edward, in his motor.

Far in a rosy mist withdrawn
   The God and all his crew,
Silenus pulled by nymphs, a faun,
   A satyr drenched in dew,

Smiled as they wept those shining tears
   Only Immortals know,
Whose feet are set among the stars,
   Above the shifting snow

And one spake out into the night,
   Before they left for ever,
" Rejoice, rejoice ! " and his great voice
   Rolled like a splendid river.

He spake in Greek, which Britons speak
   Seldom, and circumspectly ;
But Mr. Judd, that man of mud,
   Translated it correctly.

E *

And when they heard that happy word,
    Policemen leapt and ambled :
The busmen pranced, the maidens danced,
    The men in bowlers gambolled.

A wistful Echo stayed behind
    To join the mortal dances,
But Mr. Judd, with words unkind,
    Rejected her advances,

And passing down through London Town
    She stopped, for all was lonely
Attracted by a big brass plate
    Inscribed, FOR MEMBERS ONLY.

And so she went to Parliament,
    But those ungainly men
Woke up from sleep, and turned about,
    And fell asleep again.

               James Elroy Flecker.

THE BIRDS

WITHIN mankind's duration, so they say,
Khephren and Ninus lived but yesterday.
Asia had no name till man was old
And long had learned the use of iron and gold ;
And æons had passed, when the first corn was planted,
Since first the use of syllables was granted.

Men were on earth while climates slowly swung,
Fanning wide zones to heat and cold, and long
Subsidence turned great continents to sea,
And seas dried up, dried up interminably,
Age after age ; enormous seas were dried
Amid wastes of land. And the last monsters died.

Earth wore another face. O since that prime
Man with how many works has sprinkled time !
Hammering, hewing, digging tunnels, roads ;
Building ships, temples, multiform abodes.

How for his body's appetites, his toils
Have conquered all earth's products, all her soils ;
And in what thousand thousand shapes of art
He has tried to find a language for his heart !

Never at rest, never content or tired :
Insatiate wanderer, marvellously fired,
Most grandly piling and piling into the air
Stones that will topple or arch he knows not where.

And yet did I, this spring, think it more strange,
More grand, more full of awe, than all that change,
And lovely and sweet and touching unto tears,
That through man's chronicled and unchronicled years,
And even into that unguessable beyond,
The water-hen has nested by a pond,
Weaving dry flags, into a beaten floor,
The one sure product of her only lore.
Low on a ledge above the shadowed water
Then, when she heard no men, as Nature taught her,
Plashing around with busy scarlet bill
She built that nest, her nest, and builds it still.

O let your strong imagination turn
The great wheel backward, until Troy unburn,
And then unbuild, and seven Troys below
Rise out of death, and dwindle, and outflow,
Till all have passed, and none has yet been there :
Back, ever back.   Our birds still crossed the air ;
Beyond our myriad changing generations
Still built, unchanged, their known inhabitations.
A million years before Atlantis was
Our lark sprang from some hollow in the grass,
Some old soft hoof-print in a tussock's shade ;
And the wood-pigeon's smooth snow-white eggs were laid
High, amid green pines' sunset-coloured shafts,
And rooks their villages of twiggy rafts
Set on the tops of elms, where elms grew then,
And still the thumbling tit and perky wren
Popped through the tiny doors of cosy balls
And the blackbird lined with moss his high-built walls ;

A round mud cottage held the thrush's young,
And straws from the untidy sparrow's hung.
And, skimming forktailed in the evening air,
When man first was were not the martens there?
Did not those birds some human shelter crave,
And stow beneath the cornice of his cave
Their dry tight cups of clay? And from each door
Peeped on a morning wiseheads three or four.

Yes, daw and owl, curlew and crested hern,
Kingfisher, mallard, water-rail and tern,
Chaffinch and greenfinch, warbler, stonechat, ruff,
Pied wagtail, robin, fly-catcher and chough,
Missel-thrush, magpie, sparrow-hawk, and jay,
Built, those far ages gone, in this year's way.
And the first man who walked the cliffs of Rame,
As I this year, looked down and saw the same
Blotches of rusty red on ledge and cleft
With grey-green spots on them, while right and left
A dizzying tangle of gulls were floating and flying,
Wheeling and crossing and darting, crying and crying,
Circling and crying, over and over and over,
Crying with swoop and hover and fall and recover.
And below on a rock against the grey sea fretted,
Pipe-necked and stationary and silhouetted,
Cormorants stood in a wise, black, equal row
Above the nests and long blue eggs we know.

O delicate chain over all ages stretched,
O dumb tradition from what far darkness fetched:
Each little architect with its one design
Perpetual, fixed and right in stuff and line,
Each little ministrant who knows one thing,
One learned rite to celebrate the spring.
Whatever alters else on sea or shore,
These are unchanging: man must still explore.

J. C. Squire.

THE COUNTRY BEDROOM

MY room's a square and candle-lighted boat,
In the surrounding depths of night afloat.
My windows are the portholes, and the seas
The sound of rain on the dark apple-trees.

Sea monster-like beneath, an old horse blows
A snort of darkness from his sleeping nose,
Below, among drowned daisies. Far off, hark !
Far off one owl amidst the waves of dark.

Frances Cornford.

EVERYONE SANG

EVERYONE suddenly burst out singing ;
And I was filled with such delight
As prisoned birds must find in freedom
Winging wildly across the white
Orchards and dark green fields ; on ; on ; and out
   of sight.

Everyone's voice was suddenly lifted,
And beauty came like the setting sun.
My heart was shaken with tears and horror
Drifted away . . . O but every one
Was a bird ; and the song was wordless ; the
   singing will never be done.

Siegfried Sassoon.

LOST IN FRANCE

HE had the plowman's strength
In the grasp of his hand.
He could see a crow
Three miles away,
And the trout beneath the stone.
He could hear the green oats growing,
And the sou'-west making rain ;
And the wheel upon the hill
When it left the level road.
He could make a gate, and dig a pit,
And plow as straight as stone can fall.
And he is dead.   *E. R.*

THE HILL

BREATHLESS, we flung us on the windy hill,
Laughed in the sun, and kissed the lovely grass.
You said, " Through glory and ecstasy we pass ;
Wind, sun, and earth remain, the birds sing still,
When we are old, are old. . . ." " And when we die
All's over that is ours ; and life burns on
Through other lovers, other lips," said I,
" Heart of my heart, our heaven is now, is won ! "

" We are Earth's best, that learnt her lesson here.
Life is our cry. We have kept the faith ! " we said ;
" We shall go down with unreluctant tread
Rose-crowned into the darkness ! " . . . Proud we were,
And laughed, that had such brave true things to say.
—And then you suddenly cried, and turned away.

Rupert Brooke.

THE BUSY HEART

NOW that we've done our best and worst, and parted,
I would fill my mind with thoughts that will not rend.
(O heart, I do not dare go empty-hearted)
I'll think of Love in books, Love without end ;
Women with child, content ; and old men sleeping ;
And wet strong ploughlands, scarred for certain grain ;
And babes that weep, and so forget their weeping ;
And the young heavens, forgetful after rain ;
And evening hush, broken by homing wings ;
And Song's nobility, and Wisdom holy,
That live, we dead. I would think of a thousand things,
Lovely and durable, and taste them slowly,
One after one, like tasting a sweet food.
I have need to busy my heart with quietude.

Rupert Brooke.

THE DEAD

THESE hearts were woven of human joys and cares,
    Washed marvellously with sorrow, swift to mirth.
The years had given them kindness. Dawn was theirs,
    And sunset, and the colours of the earth.

These had seen movement, and heard music; known
　　Slumber and waking; loved; gone proudly friended;
Felt the quick stir of wonder; sat alone;
　　Touched flowers and furs and cheeks. All this is ended.

There are waters blown by changing winds to laughter
And lit by the rich skies, all day. And after,
　　Frost, with a gesture, stays the waves that dance
And wandering loveliness. He leaves a white
　　Unbroken glory, a gathered radiance,
A width, a shining peace, under the night.

Rupert Brooke.

TALKING WITH SOLDIERS

THE mind of the people is like mud,
　　From which arise strange and beautiful things,
But mud is none the less mud,
　　Though it bear orchids and prophesying Kings,
　　Dreams, trees, and water's bright babblings.

It has found form and colour and light,
　　The cold glimmer of the ice-wrapped Poles;
It has called a far-off glow Arcturus,
　　And some pale weeds, lilies of the valley.

It has imagined Virgil, Helen and Cassandra;
　　The sack of Troy, and the weeping for Hector—
Rearing stark up 'mid all this beauty
　　In the thick, dull neck of Ajax.

There is a dark Pine in Lapland,
　　And the great, figured Horn of the Reindeer
Moving soundlessly across the snow,
　　Is its twin brother, double-dreamed,
　　In the mind of a far-off people.

It is strange that a little mud
　　Should echo with sounds, syllables, and letters,
Should rise up and call a mountain Popocatapetl,
　　And a green-leafed wood Oleander.

These are the ghosts of invisible things;
　　There is no Lapland, no Helen and no Hector,
And the Reindeer is a darkening of the brain,
　　And Oleander is but Oleander.

Mary Magdalena and the vine Lachryma Christi,
Were like ghosts up the ghost of Vesuvius,
As I sat and drank wine with the soldiers,
As I sat in the Inn on the mountain,
Watching the shadows in my mind.

The mind of the people is like mud :
Where are the imperishable things,
The ghosts that flicker in the brain—
Silent women, orchids, and prophesying Kings,
Dreams, trees, and water's bright babblings !

W. J. Turner.

FIFTH PHILOSOPHER'S SONG

A MILLION million spermatozoa,
   All of them alive :
Out of their cataclysm but one poor Noah
   Dare hope to survive.

And among that billion minus one
   Might have chanced to be
Shakespeare, another Newton, a new Donne—
   But the One was Me.

Shame to have ousted your betters thus,
   Taking ark while the others remained outside !
Better for all of us, froward Homunculus,
   If you'd quietly died !

Aldous Huxley.

LOST LOVE

HIS eyes are quickened so with grief,
He can watch a grass or leaf
Every instant grow ; he can
Clearly through a flint wall see,
Or watch the startled spirit flee
From the throat of a dead man :
Across two counties he can hear,
And catch your words before you speak,
The woodlouse or the maggot's weak

Clamour rings in his sad ear;
And noise so slight it would surpass
Credence:—drinking sound of grass,
Worm talk, clashing jaws of moth
Chumbling holes in cloth:
The groan of ants who undertake
Gigantic loads for honour's sake,
Their sinews creak, their breath comes thin:
Whir of spiders when they spin,
And minute whispering, mumbling, sighs
Of idle grubs and flies.
This man is quickened so with grief,
He wanders god-like or like thief
Inside and out, below, above,
Without relief seeking lost love.

Robert Graves.

IN MEMORIAM D.O.M.

CHESTNUT candles are lit again
For the dead that died in spring:
Dead lovers walk the orchard ways,
And the dead cuckoos sing.

Is it they who live and we who are dead?
Hardly the springtime knows
For which to-day the cuckoo calls,
And the white blossom blows.

Listen and hear the happy wind
Whisper and lightly pass:
Your love is sweet as hawthorn is,
Your hope green as the grass.

The hawthorn's faint and quickly gone,
The grass in autumn dies;
Put by your life, and see the spring
With everlasting eyes."

William Kerr.

" Up, lord, disappoint him and cast him down."

Psalm xvii.

WISHES OF AN ELDERLY MAN

(WISHED AT A GARDEN-PARTY, JUNE, 1914)

I WISH I loved the Human Race ;
I wish I loved its silly face ;
I wish I liked the way it walks ;
I wish I liked the way it talks ;
And when I'm introduced to one
I wish I thought *What Jolly Fun !*

Walter Raleigh.

TO A LANDLORD

*Accused of neglecting one of the White Horses connected with
Alfred the Great.*

IF you have picked your lawn of leaves and snails,
If you have told your valet, even with oaths,
Once a week or so, to brush your clothes,
If you have dared to clean your teeth, or nails,
While the Horse upon the holy mountain fails—
Then God that Alfred to his earth betrothes
Send on you screaming all that honour loathes,
Horsewhipping, Hounsditch, debts, and *Daily Mails*.

Can you not even conserve ? For if indeed
The White Horse fades : then closer creeps the fight
When we shall scour the face of England white,
Plucking such men as you up like a weed,
And fling them far beyond a shaft shot right
When Wessex went to battle for the creed.

G. K. Chesterton.

117

ON GEORGE III

IN the first year of freedom's second dawn
  Died George the Third; although no tyrant, one
Who shielded tyrants, till each sense withdrawn
  Left him nor mental nor external sun:
A better farmer ne'er brush'd dew from lawn,
  A worse King never left a realm undone!
He died—but left his subjects still behind,
One half as mad—and t'other no less blind.

.   .   .   .

" God save the King!"   It is a large economy
  In God to save the like; but if He will
Be saving, all the better; for not one am I
Of those who think damnation better still.

.   .   .   .

He ever warred with freedom and the free:
  Nations as men, home subjects, foreign foes,
So that they uttered the word " Liberty!",
  Found George the Third their first opponent. Whose
History was ever stain'd as his will be
  With national and individual woes?
I grant his household abstinence, I grant
His neutral virtues, which most monarchs want;
I know he was a constant consort; own
  He was a decent sire and middling lord,
All this is much, and most upon a throne;
  His temperance, if at Apicius' board,
Is more than at an anchorite's supper shown.
  I grant him all the kindest can accord:
And this was well for him, but not for those
Millions who found him what oppression chose.

                    Byron (A Vision of Judgement).

TO SIDMOUTH AND CASTLEREAGH

AS from an ancestral oak
Two empty ravens sound their clarion,
Yell by yell, and croak by croak,
When they scent the noonday smoke
Of fresh human carrion:

As two gibbering night-birds flit
From their bowers of deadly yew
Through the night to frighten it,
When the moon is in a fit,
And the stars are none or few :

As a shark and dog-fish wait
Under an Atlantic isle,
For the negro-ship, whose freight
Is the theme of their debate,
Wrinkling their red gills the while—

Are ye, two vultures sick for battle,
Two scorpions under one wet stone,
Two bloodless wolves, whose dry throats rattle,
Two crows perched on the murrained cattle,
Two vipers tangled into one.

P. B. Shelley.

ODE

To a Pig while His Nose was being bored.

HARK ! hark ! that Pig—that Pig ! the hideous note,
  More loud, more dissonant, each moment grows—
Would one not think the knife was in his throat ?
  And yet they are only boring through his nose.

Pig ! 'tis your master's pleasure—then be still,
  And hold your nose to let the iron through !
Dare you resist your lawful Sovereign's will ?
  Rebellious Swine ! you know not what you do !

To man o'er beast the power was given ;
  Pig, hear the truth, and never murmur more !
Would you rebel against the will of Heaven ?
  You impious beast, be still, and let them bore !

The social Pig resigns his natural rights
  When first with man he covenants to live ;
He barters them for safer stye delights,
  For grains and wash, which man alone can give.

Sure is provision on the social plan,
  Secure the comforts that to each belong
Oh, happy Swine! the impartial sway of man
  Alike protects the weak Pig and the strong.

And you resist! you struggle now because
  Your master has thought fit to bore your nose!
You grunt in flat rebellion to the laws
  Society finds needful to impose!

Go to the forest, Piggy, and deplore
  The miserable lot of savage Swine!
See how young Pigs fly from the great Boar,
  And see how coarse and scantily they dine!

Behold their hourly danger, when who will
  May hunt or snare or seize them for his food!
Oh, happy Pig! whom none presumes to kill
  Till your protecting master thinks it good!

And when, at last, the closing hour of life
  Arrives (for Pigs must die as well as Man),
When in your throat you feel the long sharp knife,
  And the blood trickles to the pudding-pan;

And when, at last, the death wound yawning wide,
  Fainter and fainter grows the expiring cry,
Is there no grateful joy, no loyal pride,
  To think that for your master's good you die?

                                    Robert Southey.

BALLADE D'UNE GRANDE DAME

  HEAVEN shall forgive you Bridge at dawn,
  The clothes you wear—or do not wear—
  And Ladies' Leap-frog on the lawn
  And dyes and drugs, and *petits verres.*
  Your vicious things shall melt in air . . .
  . . . But for the Virtuous Things you do,
  The Righteous Work, the Public Care,
  It shall not be forgiven you.

120

Because you could not even yawn
When your Committees would prepare
To have the teeth of paupers drawn,
Or strip the slums of Human Hair ;
Because a Doctor Otto Maehr
Spoke of " a segregated few "—
And you sat smiling in your chair—
It shall not be forgiven you.

Though your sins cried to—Father Vaughan,
These desperate you could not spare
Who steal, with nothing left to pawn ;
You caged a man up like a bear
For ever in a jailor's care
Because his sins were more than *two* . . .
. . . I know a house in Hoxton where
It shall not be forgiven you.

ENVOI

Princess, you trapped a guileless Mayor
To meet some people that you knew . . .
When the Last Trumpet rends the air
It shall not be forgiven you.

G. K. Chesterton.

AT THE HOUSE OF MRS. KINFOOT

AT the house of Mrs. Kinfoot
Are collected
Men and women
Of all ages.
They are supposed
To sing, paint, or to play the piano.
In the drawing-room
The fireplace is set
With green tiles
Of an acanthus pattern.
The black curls of Mrs. Kinfoot
Are symmetrical.
—Descended, it is said,
From the Kings of Ethiopia—
But the British bourgeoisie has triumphed.

121

Mr. Kinfoot is bald
And talks
In front of the fireplace
With his head on one side,
And his right hand
In his pocket.
The joy of catching tame elephants,
And finding them to be white ones,
Still gleams from the jungle-eyes
Of Mrs. Kinfoot,
But her mind is no jungle
Of Ethiopia,
But a sound British meadow.

Listen then to the gospel of Mrs. Kinfoot :
" The world was made for the British bourgeoisie,
They are its Swiss Family Robinson ;
The world is not what it was.
We cannot understand all this unrest !

Adam and Eve were born to evening dress
In the southern confines
Of Belgravia.
Eve was very artistic, and all that,
And felt the fall
Quite dreadfully.
Cain was such a man of the world
And belonged to every club in London ;
His father simply adored him,
—But had never really liked Abel,
Who was rather a milk-sop.
Nothing exists which the British bourgeoisie
Does not understand ;
Therefore there is no death
—And, of course, no life.

The British bourgeoisie
Is not born,
And does not die,
But, if it is ill,
It has a frightened look in its eyes.

The War was splendid, wasn't it ?
Oh yes, splendid, splendid."

Mrs. Kinfoot is a dear,
And so artistic.

Osbert Sitwell.

" BLIGHTERS "

THE House is crammed : tier beyond tier they grin
And cackle at the Show, while prancing ranks
Of harlots shrill the chorus, drunk with din ;
" We're sure the Kaiser loves the dear old Tanks ! "
I'd like to see a Tank come down the Stalls,
Lurching to rag-time tunes, or " Home, sweet Home,"—
And there'd be no more jokes in Music-Halls
To mock the riddled corpses round Bapaume.

Siegfried Sassoon.

BASE DETAILS

IF I were fierce, and bald, and short of breath,
    I'd live with scarlet Majors at the Base,
And speed glum heroes up the line to death.
    You'd see me with my puffy petulant face,
Guzzling and gulping in the best hotel,
    Reading the Roll of Honour. " Poor young chap,"
I'd say—" I used to know his father well ;
    Yes, we've lost heavily in this last scrap."
And when the war is done and youth stone dead,
I'd toddle safely home and die—in bed.

Siegfried Sassoon.

ON A POET LAUREATE

HE had written praises of a regicide ;
    He had written praises of all kings whatever ;
He had written for republics far and wide,
    And then against them bitterer than ever ;
For pantisocracy he once had cried
    Aloud—a scheme less moral than 'twas clever ;
Then grew a hearty anti-Jacobin—
Had turn'd his coat—and would have turn'd his skin.

123

He had sung against all battles, and again
   In their high praise and glory: he had call'd
Reviewing "the ungentle craft," and then
   Become as base a critic as e'er crawl'd—
Fed, paid and pamper'd by the very men
   By whom his muse and morals had been maul'd:
He had written much blank verse, and blanker prose,
And more of both than anybody knows.

                Byron (The Vision of Judgement).

ON THE DUKE OF BUCKINGHAM

A MAN so various that he seemed to be
Not one, but all mankind's epitome.
Stiff in opinions, always in the wrong;
Was everything by starts, and nothing long;
But, in the course of one revolving moon,
Was chemist, fiddler, statesman and buffoon:
Then all for women, painting, rhyming, drinking:
Besides ten thousand freaks that died in thinking.
Blest madman, who could every hour employ,
With something new to wish, or to enjoy!
Railing and praising were his usual themes;
And both (to show his judgement) in extremes:
So over violent, or over civil,
That every man, with him, was god or devil.
In squandering wealth was his peculiar art:
Nothing went unrewarded, but desert.
Beggared by fools, whom still he found too late:
He had his jest, and they had his estate.

            John Dryden (Absalom and Ahitophel).

LINES TO A DON

REMOTE and ineffectual Don
That dared attack my Chesterton,
With that poor weapon, half-impelled,
Unlearnt, unsteady, hardly held,
Unworthy for a tilt with men—
Your quavering and corroded pen;

Don poor at Bed and worse at Table,
Don pinched, Don starved, Don miserable ;
Don stuttering, Don with roving eyes,
Don nervous, Don of crudities ;
Don clerical, Don ordinary,
Don self-absorbed and solitary ;
Don here-and-there, Don epileptic ;
Don puffed and empty, Don dyspeptic ;
Don middle-class, Don sycophantic,
Don dull, Don brutish, Don pedantic ;
Don hypocritical, Don bad,
Don furtive, Don three-quarters mad ;
Don (since a man must make an end)
Don that shall never be my friend.

      .   .   .

Don different from those regal Dons !
With hearts of gold and lungs of bronze,
Who shout and bang and roar and bawl
The Absolute across the hall,
Or sail in amply bellowing gown
Enormous through the Sacred Town,
Bearing from College to their homes
Deep cargoes of gigantic tomes ;
Dons admirable !   Dons of Might !
Uprising on my inward sight
Compact of ancient tales, and port
And sleep—and learning of a sort.
Dons English, worthy of the land ;
Dons rooted ; Dons that understand.
Good Dons perpetual that remain
A landmark, walling in the plain—
The horizon of my memories—
Like large and comfortable trees.

      .   .   .

Don very much apart from these,
Thou scapegoat Don, thou Don devoted,
Don to thine own damnation quoted
Perplexed to find thy trivial name
Reared in my verse to lasting shame.

Don dreadful, rasping Don and wearing,
Repulsive Don—Don past all bearing.
Don of the cold and doubtful breath,
Don despicable, Don of death ;
Don nasty, skimpy, silent, level ;
Don evil ; Don that serves the devil.
Don ugly—that makes fifty lines.
There is a Canon which confines
A Rhymed Octosyllabic Curse
If written in Iambic Verse
To fifty lines.   I never cut ;
I far prefer to end it—but
Believe me I shall soon return.
My fires are banked, but still they burn
To write some more about the Don
That dared attack my Chesterton.

Hilaire Belloc.

THE NUN'S LAMENT FOR PHILIP SPARROW

WHEN I remember'd again
How my Philip was slain,
I wept and I wailed,
The tears down hailed ;
But nothing it avail'd
To call Philip again
Whom Gib our cat hath slain.
Heu, heu, me,
That I am woe for thee !
Levavi oculos meos in montis ;
Would that I had Xenophontis
Or Socrates the Wise,
To show me their device
Moderately to take
This sorrow that I make
For Philip Sparrow's sake !
It had a velvet cap,
And would sit on my lap,
And seek after small worms,
And sometimes white bread crumbs ;
And many times and oft

Within my breast soft
It would lie and rest.
   Sometimes he would gasp
When he saw a wasp ;
A fly or a gnat,
He would fly at that ;
And prettily he would pant
When he saw an ant ;
Lord, how he would pry
After the butterfly !
Lord, how he would hop
After the grasshop !
And when I said, Phip, Phip,
Then he would leap and skip,
And take me by the lip.
   De profundis clamavi
When I saw my sparrow die.
   Vengeance I ask and cry,
By way of exclamation,
On all the whole nation
Of cats wild and tame ;
That cat especially
   That slew so cruelly
My little pretty sparrow
That I brought up at Carow.
   O cat of churlish kind,
The fiend was in thy mind.
I would thou hadst been blind !
The leopards savage,
The lions in their rage,
May they catch thee in their paws,
And gnaw thee in their jaws ;
The dragons with their tongues
May they poison thy liver and lungs.
Of India the greedy gripes
May they tear out all thy tripes ;
Of Arcady the bears
May they pluck away thine ears ;
The wild wolf Lycaon
Bite asunder thy back-bone ;
Of Ætna the burning hill,

That night and day burneth still,
Set thy tail in a blaze,
That all the world may gaze
And wonder upon thee,
From Ocean, the great sea,
Unto the Isles of Orchadye ;
From Tilbury Ferry
To the plain of Salisbury.

J. Skelton.

A PORTRAIT

I A M a kind of farthing dip,
    Unfriendly to the nose and eyes ;
A blue-behinded ape, I skip
    Upon the trees of Paradise.

At mankind's feast I take my place
    In solemn sanctimonious state,
And have the air of saying grace
    While I defile the dinner plate.

I am " the smiler with the knife,"
    The battener upon garbage, I—
Dear Heaven, with such a rancid life,
    Were it not better far to die ?

Yet still, about the human pale,
    I love to scamper, love to race,
To swing by my irreverent tail
    All over the most holy place ;

And when at length, some golden day,
    The unfailing sportsman, aiming at,
Shall bag me—all the world shall say :
    Thank God, and there's an end of that !

R. L. Stevenson.

TO EDWARD FITZGERALD

I CHANCED upon a new book yesterday :
I opened it, and, where my finger lay
  'Twixt page and uncut page, these words I read
  —Some six or seven at most—and learned thereby
That you, Fitzgerald, whom by ear and eye
She never knew, " thanked God my wife was dead."
Ay, dead ! and were yourself alive, good Fitz,
How to return you thanks would task my wits :
  Kicking you seems the common lot of curs—
  While more appropriate greeting lends you grace :
Surely to spit there glorifies your face—
  Spitting from lips once sanctified by Hers.
Robert Browning.

CROMEK

  A PETTY sneaking knave I knew—
  O! Mr. Cromek, how do ye do?
William Blake.

NORA CRIONA

I HAVE looked him round and looked him through,
Know everything that he will do
In such a case, and such a case,
And when a frown comes on his face
I dream of it, and when a smile
I trace its sources in a while.

He cannot do a thing but I
Peep to find the reason why,
For I love him, and I seek,
Every evening in the week,
To peep behind his frowning eye
With little query, little pry,
And make him if a woman can
Happier than any man.

Yesterday he gripped her tight
And cut her throat—and serve her right !
James Stephens.

F

TO A FAT LADY SEEN FROM THE TRAIN

O WHY do you walk through the fields in gloves,
    Missing so much and so much ?
O fat white woman whom nobody loves,
Why do you walk through the fields in gloves,
When the grass is soft as the breast of doves
    And shivering-sweet to the touch ?
O why do you walk through the fields in gloves,
    Missing so much and so much ?

Frances Cornford.

A PSALM OF MONTREAL

THE *City of Montreal is one of the most rising and, in many respects, most agreeable on the American continent, but its inhabitants are as yet too busy with commerce to care greatly about the masterpieces of old Greek Art. In the Montreal Museum of Natural History I came upon two plaster casts, one of the Antinous and the other of the Discobolus—not the good one, but in my poem, of course, I intend the good one— banished from public view to a room where were all manner of skins, plants, snakes, insects, etc., and, in the middle of these, an old man stuffing an owl.*

"*Ah,*" *said I,* "*so you have some antiques here ; why don't you put them where people can see them ?* "

"*Well, sir,*" *answered the custodian,* "*you see they are rather vulgar.*"

He then talked a great deal and said his brother did all Mr. Spurgeon's printing.

The dialogue—perhaps true, perhaps imaginary, perhaps a little of the one and a little of the other—between the writer and this old man gave rise to the lines that follow :

Stowed away in a Montreal lumber room
The Discobolus standeth and turneth his face to the wall ;
Dusty, cobweb-covered, maimed and set at naught,
Beauty crieth in an attic and no man regardeth :
              O God ! O Montreal !

Beautiful by night and day, beautiful in summer and in
    winter,
Whole or maimed, always and alike beautiful—

He preacheth gospel of grace to the skin of owls
And to one who seasoneth the skins of Canadian owls :
O God ! O Montreal !

When I saw him I was wroth and I said, " O Discobolus !
Beautiful Discobolus, a Prince both among gods and men !
What doest thou here, how camest thou hither, Discobolus,
Preaching thy gospel in vain to the skins of owls ? "
O God ! O Montreal !

And I turned to the man of skins and said unto him, " O
thou man of skins,
Wherefore hast thou done thus to shame the beauty of the
Discobolus ? "
But the Lord had hardened the heart of the man of skins
And he answered, " My brother-in-law is haberdasher to
Mr. Spurgeon."
O God ! O Montreal !

" The Discobolus is put here because he is vulgar—
He has neither vest nor pants with which to cover his limbs ;
I, Sir, am a person of most respectable connections—
My brother-in-law is haberdasher to Mr. Spurgeon."
O God ! O Montreal !

Then I said, " O brother-in-law to Mr. Spurgeon's haber-
dasher,
Who seasonest also the skins of Canadian owls,
Thou callest trousers ' pants,' whereas I call them ' trousers,'
Therefore thou art in hell-fire and may the Lord pity thee !"
O God ! O Montreal !

" Preferrest thou the gospel of Montreal to the gospel of
Hellas,
The gospel of thy connection with Mr. Spurgeon's haber-
dashery to the gospel of the Discobolus ? "
Yet none the less blasphemed he beauty saying, " The
Discobolus hath no gospel,
But my brother-in-law is haberdasher to Mr. Spurgeon."
O God ! O Montreal !

Samuel Butler.

SOLILOQUY OF THE SPANISH CLOISTER

G R - R - R - there go, my heart's abhorrence !
    Water your damned flower-pots, do !
If hate killed men, Brother Lawrence,
    God's blood, would not mine kill you !
What ? your myrtle-bush wants trimming ?
    Oh, that rose has prior claims—
Needs its leaden vase filled brimming ?
    Hell dry you up with its flames !

At the meal we sit together ;
    Salve tibi ! I must hear
Wise talk of the kind of weather,
    Sort of season, time of year :
Not a plenteous cork-crop : scarcely
    Dare we hope oak-galls, I doubt ;
What's the Latin name for " parsley " ?
    What's the Greek name for Swine's Snout ?

Whew ! We'll have our platter burnished,
    Laid with care on our own shelf !
With a fire-new spoon we're furnished,
    And a goblet for ourself,
Rinsed like something sacrificial
    Ere 'tis fit to touch our chaps—
Marked with L. for our initial !
    (He-he ! There his lily snaps !)

Saint, forsooth ! While brown Dolores
    Squats outside the Convent bank
With Sanchicha, telling stories,
    Steeping tresses in the tank,
Blue-black, lustrous, thick like horsehairs,
    —Can't I see his dead eye glow,
Bright as 'twere a Barbary corsair's ?
    (That is, if he'd let it show !)

When he finishes refection,
    Knife and fork he never lays
Cross-wise, to my recollection,
    As do I, in Jesu's praise.

I, the Trinity illustrate,
    Drinking watered orange-pulp—
In three sips the Arian frustrate;
    While he drains his at one gulp!

Oh, those melons! If he's able
    We're to have a feast; so nice!
One goes to the Abbot's table,
    All of us get each a slice.
How go on your flowers? None double?
    Not one fruit-sort can you spy?
Strange!—And I, too, at such trouble,
    Keep them close-nipped on the sly!

There's a great text in Galatians,
    Once you trip on it, entails
Twenty-nine distinct damnations,
    One sure, if another fails;
If I trip him just a-dying,
    Sure of heaven as sure can be,
Spin him round and send him flying
    Off to hell, a Manichee?

Or, my scrofulous French novel
    On grey paper with blunt type!
Simply glance at it, you grovel
    Hand and foot in Belial's gripe;
If I double down its pages
    At the woeful sixteenth print,
When he gathers his greengages,
    Ope a sieve and slip it in't?

Or, there's Satan!—one might venture
    Pledge one's soul to him, yet leave
Such a flaw in the indenture
    As he'd miss till, past retrieve,
Blasted lay that rose-acacia
    We're so proud of! *Hy, Zy, Hine.* . . .
'St, there's Vespers! *Plena gratia*
    Ave, Virgo! Gr-r-r—you swine!

Robert Browning.

THE CURSE

WHOEVER guesses, thinks, or dreams he knows
Who is my mistress, wither by this curse ;
      Him, only for his purse,
      May some dull whore to love dispose,
And she yield then to all that are his foes ;
   May he be scorned by one, whom all else scorn,
   Forswear to others, what to her he hath sworn,
   With fear of missing, shame of getting, torn.

Madness his sorrow, gout his cramp, may he
Make, by but thinking, who hath made him such ;
      And may he feel no touch
      Of conscience, but of fame, and be
Anguished, not that 'twas sin, but that 'twas she ;
   In early and long scarceness may he rot,
   For land which had been his, if he had not
   Himself incestuously an heir begot.

May he dream treason, and believe that he
Meant to perform it, and confess, and die,
      And no record tell why ;
      His sons, which none of his may be,
Inherit nothing but his infamy ;
   Or may he so long parasites have fed,
   That he would fain be theirs whom he hath bred,
   And at the last be circumcised for bread.

The venom of all stepdames, gamesters' gall,
What tyrants and their subjects interwish,
      What plants, mines, beasts, fowl, fish,
      Can contribute, all ill which all
Prophets or poets spake, and all which shall
   Be annexed in schedules unto this by me,
   Fall on that man ; for if it be a she
   Nature beforehand hath out-cursed me.

                    John Donne.

"*O Britain's Representatives (Renown'd*
Like her, for Pow'r with gen'rous Goodness crown'd)
Permit the Transports of a British *Muse*
And pardon Raptures that yourselves infuse."

NAHUM TATE, Poet Laureate, on the
New Parliament (1701).

TO THE KING (CHARLES I) AND QUEEN
UPON THEIR UNHAPPY DISTANCES

W O E, woe to them, who (by a ball of strife)
Doe, and have parted here a Man and Wife:
CHARLS the best Husband, while MARIA strives
To be, and is, the very best of Wives:
Like Streams, you are divorc'd; but 'twill come when
These eyes of mine shall see you mix agen.
Thus speaks the Oke, here; C. and M. shall meet,
Treading on Amber, with their silver-feet:
Nor wil't be long, ere this accomplish'd be;
The words found true, C.M. remember me.

Robert Herrick.

TO THE QUEEN
[OF CHARLES I]

T H O U great commandress, that dost move
Thy sceptre o'er the crown of Love,
And through his empire, with the awe
Of thy chaste beams, dost give the law;
From his profaner altars we
Turn to adore thy deity:
He only can wild lust provoke,
Thou those impurer flames canst choke;
And where he scatters looser fires,
Thou turn'st them into chaste desires;
His kingdom knows no rule but this,
Whatever pleaseth, lawful is;
Thy sacred lore shows us the path
Of modesty and constant faith,
Which makes the rude male satisfied
With one fair female by his side;
Doth either sex to each unite,
And form Love's pure hermaphrodite,
To this thy faith, behold the wild

F*

Satyr already reconciled,
Who from the influence of thine eye
Hath suck'd the deep divinity.
O free them then, that they may teach
The Centaur and the horse-man, preach
To beasts and birds, sweetly to rest
Each in his proper lair and nest;
They shall convey it to the flood,
Till there thy law be understood:
    So shalt thou with thy pregnant fire
    The water, earth, and air inspire.

Thomas Carew.

GREAT BRITAIN'S GLORY
A Poem

ASPIRING Muse, commence a Noble Flight,
And strike thy joyful Wings in open Light;
New string thy Harp, and Tune thy chearful Lays,
To sacred GEORGE, and great AUGUSTUS Praise;
In sounds to move the Ravisht *Hermon's* Hill,
And faster make the *Gilead-Balm* distil.

Come BRITAINS, you whom needless Fears possess
See how kind Heav'n confirms your Happiness:
Behold Great GEORGE, the Sacred Promis'd Prince,
Whom Wond'rous Prophets many Ages since Foretold:
" That when the Mystick Figures of the Year
" To such a certain Number should Amount
" (As fill this present Lucky Year's Account,)
" O'er *England* there should Reign a shining Star,
" Of that Divine, and Gracious Influence,
" Should make Proud Neighb'ring Nations Fear;
" And mightier *Britain's* Happy Genius prove,
" Blessing the Land with Plenty, Peace, and Love.
'Tis You, O *Sacred Sir*, for Empire Born,
That makes this Strange and Great Prediction true;
And yet another Miracle perform,
'Tis *You* shall make us Blest, and make us own it too!

  .   .   .   .

All Hail, Great KING! Whom ev'ry Miracle,
Has still Preserv'd for *Universal Rule!*

Thou Mighty *Fabius* of a Mournful State,
Whom Heav'n hath sent i'th' Crisis of our Fate!
We bless the Winds, and Waves, and Flowing Tide,
That did Espouse and Battle on thy Side,
And ev'ry Smiling and Conspiring Gale,
That did impregnate the Extended Sail:
We bless th' *Almighty's* Steady Pow'rful Hand,
That held the Rudder, till the *Bark* did Land;
The Happy *Bark*, that all our Blessings brought,
Charg'd with thy Self and Son, a doubly Royal Fraught.

But see, the Mighty *Hero* now draws near,   )
Loud *Io Pæons* glad the Ecchoing Air,   }
And Troops of Vig'rous Youth his joyful Way prepare.)
See, how beneath his large extensive Shade,
Th' oppress'd and Languid at Repose are laid!
Whilst Aged Parents his just Praise Proclaim,
And untaught Stam'ring Infants Bless his Name!
A Gen'ral Joy springs up in ev'ry Face,
And all Mankind meets with Distinguisht Grace.
O may each Rising Sun his *Age* Renew,
And each Revolving Morn fresh *Triumphs* View!
May Blooming *Honours*, as His Years Increase;
Our Sacred *Guide* in *War*, and *Guard* in *Peace!*
And oh, Thou ever *Blest!*   Now to my Pray'rs incline
For *Him*, whose *Fame* and *Glory* best resembles Thine!

But now I draw the Veil. . . . The Dazzling Light
Of Glory, Shines too Heavenly Fierce and Bright!
Yet never shall my *Muse*, my K I N G forget,
The Pension of a Prince's Praise is great!
'Tis the Bright Bullion of the Shining Mind:
'Tis like the Work of G O D, in *Man* Refin'd!
What Heav'n to Saints, the same do K I N G S below,
Alike these Blessings, and their Gifts bestow:
Mercy in both's the Type of Sacred Grace,
And shows the *Monarch's* Born of Heav'nly Race!
Long may *He* Shine, and spread his Beams as far,
As from the Morning to the Evening Star;
Till His convincing Rays His Foes o'ercome,
And for his *Glorious Magnitude*, the Scanted Globe want
    room!   *Joseph Harris* (1680–1729.)

BIRTHDAY ODE, 1732

LET there be light!
Such was at once the word and work of heav'n,
    When from the void of universal night
    Free nature sprung to the Creator's sight,
And day to glad the new-born world was giv'n.

Succeeding days to ages roll'd,
And ev'ry age some wonder told:
At length arose this glorious morn!
    When, to extend his bounteous pow'r,
    High heav'n announc'd this instant hour
The best of monarchs shall be born!

    Born to protect and bless the land!
And while the laws his people form,
His scepter glories to confirm
    Their wishes are his sole command.

The word that form'd the world
    In vain did make mankind;
Unless, his passions to restrain,
    Almighty wisdom had design'd
Sometimes a WILLIAM or a GEORGE should reign.
Yet farther, *Britons,* cast your eyes,
Behold a long succession rise
Of future fair felicities.

    Around the royal table spread,
See how the beauteous branches shine!
    Sprung from the fertile genial bed
Of glorious GEORGE and CAROLINE.
                Colley Cibber (Poet Laureate).

ON THE LATE QUEEN'S SICKNESS AND DEATH

SAY, Muse, if Sighs will give thee leave,
For thou hast ample Cause to grieve,
Th' Alarm united Kingdoms took,
Th' Emotions which each Bosom shook,
The wild Distress, unceasing Moan,
The weeping Eye, heart-breaking Groan,

In every Corner heard and seen,
When late our darling *Caroline*,
Britannia's, and her King's Delight,
The Joy of every Subject's Sight,
Oppress'd with mortal Sickness lay:

What Pen th' Amazement can display,
Or Tongue describe the piercing Grief,
When Physick's Aid brought no Relief,
And *George* with all his blooming Race,
Tears trickling down each Royal Face,
Regardless of their Health and Rest,
Contended which should nurse her best,
Eager with pious Zeal to save
The Wife, the Mother, from the Grave?

.   .   .   .   .   .

Deep-piercing was the rude Alarm,
When she, who wont our Eyes to charm,
Our Ears with Musick to rejoice
When e'er she deigned to lift her Voice,
Who with a Smile each Heart could win,
Tho' Disappointment rag'd within,
Who with a Word could Passion chain,
And render all its Fury vain,
Withdrawn, and languishing in Bed,
Was more than once reported dead.

The News attended with less Woe
Had been of an invading Foe.
But if, while this Event we fear'd,
Some glimpse of flattering Hope appear'd,
How soon to Rapture turn'd Despair,
As when o'ercast the dusky Air
At once grows brighter than a Ray,
Shot from th' effulgent Source of Day!
New Life in every Face was seen,
And more erect each alter'd Mein.

But, ah! how false is *Syren*-Joy,
That flatters only to destroy,

141

And, as when Fevers intermit,
Holds but till next returning Fit.
Then Hope with all its chearful Train,
Like Tides at Ebb, flows back again.

· · · · · ·

Yet, e're her native Skies the Queen
Rejoin'd, how moving was the Scene!
How tender was the last Adieu,
When round her Bed a Glance she threw,
And saw her Lord, the Kingdom's Chief,
Dissolv'd in Tears, and dumb with Grief,
Attended with his numerous Line,
In whom a Thousand Graces shine,
But then so chang'd with haggard Woe,
Scarce could she her own off-spring know.

Like *Niobe*, one Speechless stood,
Insensible as Stone or Wood.
Her Anguish took a Root so deep,
She look'd amaz'd, but could not weep,
As if Affliction's wonted Train
Were inexpressive of her Pain.
Another, seiz'd with mortal Fright,
Sunk Lifeless at the killing Sight.
The Rest, in various Shapes, impart
The Symptoms of a wounded Heart.

· · · · · ·

Hast thou not equal Cause to mourn
O'er *Carolina's* sacred Urn,
Thou self-tormented Isle, for she
A nursing Mother was to Thee?
Say then, what monumental Praise,
What Trophy do'st Thou mean to raise
For her, who with a Parent's View
Was once thy Queen and Guardian too?
If Honour, Safety, Truth you prize,
The following Scheme will best advise.

Henceforth let Party-Fury cease,
The Worm that prays upon your Peace.

Anonymous, 1738.

142

TO THE INFANT PRINCESS ROYAL

WELCOME, bud beside the rose,
On whose stem our safety grows ;
Welcome, little Saxon Guelph ;
Welcome for thine own small self ;
Welcome for thy father, mother,
Proud the one and safe the other ;
Welcome to three kingdoms ; nay,
Such is thy potential day,
Welcome, little mighty birth,
To our human star the earth.

Some have wish'd thee boy ; and some
Gladly wait till boy shall come,
Counting it a genial sign
When a lady leads the line.
What imports it, girl or boy :
England's old historic joy
Well might be content to see
Queens alone come after thee,—
Twenty visions of thy mother
Following sceptred, each the other,
Linking with their roses white
Ages of unborn delight.
What imports it who shall lead,
So that the good line succeed ?
So that love and peace feel sure
Of old hate's discomfiture ?
Thee appearing by the rose
Safety comes, and peril goes ;
Thee appearing, earth's new spring
Fears no winter's " grisly king " ;
Hope anew leaps up, and dances
In the hearts of human chances :
France, the brave, but too quick-blooded,
Wisely has her threat re-studied ;
England now, as safe as she
From the strifes that need not be,
And the realms thus hush'd and still,
Earth with fragrant thought may fill,

Growing harvests of all good,
Day by day, as planet should,
Till it clap its hands and cry,
Hail, matur'd humanity !
Earth has outgrown want and war ;
Earth is now no childish star.

But behold, where thou dost lie,
Heeding nought, remote or nigh !
Nought of all the news we sing
Dost thou know, sweet ignorant thing ;
Nought of planet's love, nor people's :
Nor dost hear the giddy steeples
Carolling of thee and thine,
As if heav'n had rain'd them wine :

    .   .   .

Nor dost know thy very mother's
Balmy bosom from another's,
Though thy small blind lips pursue it,
Nor the arms that draw thee to it,
Nor the eyes, that, while they fold thee,
Never can enough behold thee.
Mother true and good has she,
Little strong one, been to thee,
Nor with listless indoor ways
Weaken'd thee for future days ;
But has done her strenuous duty
To thy brain and to thy beauty,
Till thou cam'st, a blossom bright,
Worth the kiss of air and light ;
To thy healthy self a pleasure ;
To the world a balm and treasure.

Leigh Hunt.

ODE SUNG AT THE EXHIBITION, 1862

UPLIFT a thousand voices full and sweet,
    In this wide hall with earth's invention stor'd,
    And praise th' invisible universal Lord,
Who lets once more in peace the nations meet,
    Where, Science, Art, and Labour have outpour'd
Their myriad horns of plenty at our feet.

O silent father of our Kings to be,
Mourn'd in this golden hour of jubilee,
For this, for all, we weep our thanks to thee!

The world-compelling plan was thine,
And, lo! the long laborious miles
Of Palace; lo! the giant aisles,
    Rich in model and design;
Harvest-tool and husbandry,
Loom, and wheel, and engin'ry,
    Secrets of the sullen mine,
    Steel and gold, and corn and wine,
    Fabric rough, or fairy fine,
    Sunny tokens of the Line,
Polar marvels, and a feast
Of wonder, out of West and East,
    And shapes and hues of Art divine!
All of beauty, all of use
That one fair planet can produce,
    Brought from under every star,
Blown from over every main,
And mixt, as life is mixt with pain,
    The works of peace with works of war.
War himself must make alliance
With rough Labour and fine Science,
Else he would but strike in vain.

And is the goal so far away?
Far, how far, no tongue can say:
Let us have our dream to-day.

O ye, the wise who think, the wise who reign,
From growing Commerce loose her latest chain,
And let the fair, white-winged peacemaker fly
To happy havens under all the sky,
And mix the seasons and the golden hours,
Till each man find his own in all men's good,
And all men work in noble brotherhood,
Breaking their mailed fleets and armed towers,
And ruling by obeying nature's powers,
And gathering all the fruits of Peace and crown'd
    with all her flowers.

Alfred, Lord Tennyson (*Poet Laureate*).

145

MAFEKING
OCTOBER 15, 1899 TO MAY 16, 1900

ONCE again, banners, fly!
Clang again, bells, on high,
Sounding to sea and sky,
    Longer and louder,
Mafeking's glory with
Kimberley, Ladysmith,
Of our unconquered Kith
    Prouder and prouder.

Hemmed in for half a year,
Still with no succour near,
Nor word of hope to cheer
    Wounded and dying,
Famished, and foiled of sleep
By the fierce cannon's leap,
They vowed still, still to keep
    England's Flag flying.

Nor was their mettle shown
By male and strong alone,
But, as intrepid grown,
    Fragile and tender,
Without or tear or sigh,
Echoed the brave old cry,
" We, too, would rather die,
    Die than surrender."

As pressed the foe more near,
Only with naked spear,
Ne'er knowing what to fear,
    Parley, or blench meant,
Forward through shot and shell,
While still the foremost fell,
They with resistless yell
    Stormed his intrenchment

Then, when hope dawned at last
And fled the foe, aghast
At the relieving blast
    Heard in the melley,—
O our stout, stubborn kith!

Kimberley, Ladysmith,
Mafeking, wedded with
      Lucknow and Delhi!

Sound for them martial lay!
Crown them with battle-bay,
Both those who died, and they
      'Gainst death could wrestle.
Powell of endless fame,
All, all with equal claim,
And, of the storied name,
      Gallant young Cecil!

Long as the waves shall roll,
Long as Fame guards her scroll,
And men through heart and soul
      Thrill to true glory,
Their deed, from age to age,
Shall voice and verse engage,
Swelling the splendid page
      Of England's Story.
                Alfred Austin (*Poet Laureate*).

ON THE DEATH OF KING EDWARD VII

THE will of God we must obey.
Dreadful—our King taken away!
The greatest friend of the nation,
Mighty monarch and protection!

Heavenly Father, help in sorrow
Queen-Mother, and them to follow,
What to do without him who has gone!
Pray help! help! and do lead us on.

Greatest sorrow England ever had
When death took away our dear Dad;
A king was he from head to sole,
Loved by his people one and all.

His mighty work for the Nation,
Making peace and strengthening Union—
Always at it since on the throne:
Saved the country more than one billion.
           Broadsheet sold in London streets
           at King Edward's funeral.

147

EPIGRAMS

" A box where sweets compacted lie."

George Herbert.

EPIGRAMS

A CURE FOR POETRY
S E V E N wealthy towns contend for Homer dead
Thro' which the living Homer beg'd his bread.
Thomas Seward (from *John Heywood*).

THE MODERN POET (1925)
W I T H what small pains procures the poet now
A wreath of bays with which to deck his brow;
For two things only can obscure his fame—
A love of beauty or a sense of shame.   *Sylvis.*

OF TREASON
T R E A S O N doth never prosper; what's the reason?
For if it prosper, none dare call it treason.
John Harington.

ON A BEAUTIFUL YOUTH STRUCK BLIND WITH LIGHTNING
S U R E, 'twas by Providence design'd
  Rather in pity than in hate,
That he should be, like Cupid, blind,
  To save him from Narcissus' fate.   *O. Goldsmith.*

THE FIVE REASONS FOR DRINKING
I F all be true that I do think,
  There are five reasons we should drink;
  Good wine—a friend—or being dry—
  Or lest we should be by and by—
  Or any other reason why.   *Henry Aldrich.*

BURLESQUE
I F the man who turnips cries,
  Cry not when his father dies,
  'Tis a proof that he had rather
  Have a turnip than his father.
Samuel Johnson.

EPIGRAMS
THE KISS

" I S A W you take his kiss ! "   " 'Tis true."
" O, modesty ! "   " 'Twas strictly kept :
    He thought me asleep : at least, I knew
    He thought I thought he thought I slept."

Coventry Patmore.

CHLOE

B R I G H T as the day, and like the morning fair,
Such Chloe is—and common as the air.

Lansdowne.

ON LADY POLTAGRUE, A PUBLIC PERIL

T H E Devil, having nothing else to do,
Went off to tempt My Lady Poltagrue.
My Lady, tempted by a private whim,
To his extreme annoyance, tempted him.

H. Belloc.

ON AN UPRIGHT JUDGE

I N church your grandsire cut his throat ;
To do the job too long he tarried :
He should have had my heart vote
To cut his throat before he married.

Jonathan Swift.

ON CHARLES II

H E R E lies our sovereign Lord the King,
    Whose word no man relies on,
Who never said a foolish thing
    Nor ever did a wise one.

Rochester.

ON PETER ROBINSON

H E R E lies the preacher, judge and poet, Peter,
Who broke the laws of God, and man, and metre.

Francis Jeffrey.

152

EPIGRAMS

ON A CERTAIN LORD'S GIVING SOME THOUSAND POUNDS FOR A HOUSE

s o many thousands for a house
For you, of all the world, Lord Mouse!
A little house would best accord
With you, my very little lord!
And then exactly match'd would be
Your house and hospitality.

David Garrick.

DOCTOR FELL

I D O not love thee, Doctor Fell;
The reason why I cannot tell.
But this I'm sure I know full well,
I do not love thee, Doctor Fell.

T. Brown (from *Martial*).

THE CHOSEN PEOPLE

H O w odd
Of God
To choose
The Jews.

W. N. Ewer.

FOOLS—AND FOOLS

A N S W E R not a fool according to his folly,
Lest thou also be like unto him.

Answer a fool according to his folly,
Lest he be wise in his own conceit.

The Authorised Version.

EPIGRAM

S I R , I admit your general rule,
That every poet is a fool:
But you yourself may serve to show it,
That every fool is not a poet.

Matthew Prior.

THE MAIDEN'S CHOICE

A F O O L and knave with different views,
  For Julia's hand apply :
The knave, to mend his fortune sues,
  The fool, to please his eye.

Ask you, how Julia will behave ?
  Depend on't for a rule,
If she's a fool, she'll wed the knave—
  If she's a knave, the fool.   *S. Bishop.*

A RIDDLE SOLVED

K I N D souls, you wonder why, love you,
When you, you wonder why, love none.
We love, Fool, for the good we do,
Not that which unto us is done !

                              Coventry Patmore.

ETERNITY

H E who bends to himself a Joy
Doth the wingèd life destroy ;
But he who kisses the Joy as it flies
Lives in Eternity's sunrise.   *W. Blake.*

THE LADY WHO OFFERS HER LOOKING-GLASS TO VENUS

V E N U S , take my votive glass ;
Since I am not what I was,
What from this day I shall be,
Venus, let me never see.

            Matthew Prior (from *Ausonius*).

TO SILENCE

W H Y the warning finger-tip
Pressed for ever on thy lip ?
To remind the pilgrim Sound
That it moves on holy ground,
In a breathing-space to be
Hushed for all eternity.   *J. B. Tabb.*

EPIGRAMS
RESPICE FINEM

M Y soul, sit thou a patient looker-on;
Judge not the play before the play is done:
Her plot hath many changes; every day
Speaks a new scene; the last act crowns the play.

Francis Quarles.

DUSTING

T H E dust comes secretly day after day,
Lies on my ledge and dulls my shining things.
But O this dust that I shall drive away
    Is flowers and kings,
Is Solomon's temple, poets, Nineveh.

Viola Meynell.

ON HIS SEVENTY-FIFTH BIRTHDAY

I S T R O V E with none; for none was worth my strife.
Nature I loved and, next to Nature, Art;
    I warmed both hands before the fire of life;
It sinks, and I am ready to depart.

W. S. Landor.

DIRCE

S T A N D close around, ye Stygian set,
    With Dirce in one boat conveyed,
Or Charon, seeing, may forget
    That he is old and she a shade.

W. S. Landor.

ON THE PHRASE, "TO KILL TIME"

T H E R E ' S scarce a point whereon mankind agree
So well, as in their boast of killing me:
I boast of nothing, but, when I've a mind,
I think I can be even with mankind.

From *Voltaire : Dodd's* Select Epigrams.

MY OWN EPITAPH

L I F E is jest, and all things show it;
I thought so once, but now I know it.

John Gay.

EPITAPH

HERE lie I, Martin Elginbrodde :
Ha'e mercy o' my soul, Lord God,
As I wad do, were I Lord God
And ye were Martin Elginbrodde.

From an *Aberdeen tombstone.*

UPON A CHILD

HERE a pretty baby lies
Sung asleep with lullabies ;
Pray be silent, and not stir
Th' easy earth that covers her. *R. Herrick.*

ON THE DEATH OF SIR ALBERTUS AND LADY MORTON

HE first deceas'd—she, for a little, try'd
To live without him, lik'd it not and dy'd.

Henry Wotton.

THE BETTER WAY

IF you desire to paralyse
Your enemy, don't " damn his eyes " ;
From futile blasphemy desist ;
Send him to Blank the oculist.

Walter Leaf (from *Nicarchus*).

THE MODERN WORLD (1925)

STRANGER, here lies that one time 'modern' world,
That noble and courageous age which hurled
Its gauntlet in the very teeth of fate
And dared and died—What are you laughing at ? *E. S.*

EPITAPH BY A SON

BENEATH this stone, in hopes of Zion,
Doth lie the landlord of the Lion ;
His son keeps on the business still,
Resigned unto the heavenly will.

From *Fairley's Epitaphiana.*

EPIGRAMS

EMINENT PHYSICISTS

I

N A T U R E , and Nature's laws, lay hid in night :
God said, *Let Newton be !* and all was light.

A. Pope.

II

I T did not last : the Devil, howling *Ho !*
Let Einstein be ! restored the status quo.

J. C. Squire.

RELATIVITY

T H E R E was a young lady named Bright
Who would travel much faster than light.
   She started one day
   In the relative way,
And came back the previous night.

Anonymous.

THE MENDELIAN THEORY

T H E R E was a young fellow called Starky
Who had an affair with a darky.
   The result of his sins
   Was quadruplets, not twins :
One black, and one white, and two khaki.

Anonymous.

THE JUNG IDEA

T H E young things who frequent picture-palaces
Have no use for this psycho-analysis ;
   And although Doctor Freud
   Is distinctly annoyed
They cling to their old-fashioned fallacies.   *P. H.*

ON MONSIEUR COUÉ

T H I S very remarkable man
Commends a most practical plan ;
   You can do what you want
   If you don't think you can't
So don't think you can't think you can.

Charles Inge.

MIND OVER MATTER

T H E R E was a faith-healer of Deal
Who said, " Although pain isn't real,
  If I sit on a pin
  And it punctures my skin
I dislike what I fancy I feel."   *Anonymous.*

MATERIALISM

T H E R E was a professor of Beaulieu
Who said mind was matter or ὕλη,
  This contempt for the εἶδος ;
  Though common at Cnidos
Distressed the New Forest unduly.

C. E. M. Joad.

IDEALISM

T H E R E once was a man who said " God
Must think it exceedingly odd
  If he finds that this tree
  Continues to be
When there's no one about in the Quad."

Ronald Knox.

A REPLY

D E A R S I R ,
      Your astonishment's odd :
I am always about in the Quad.
      And that's why the tree
      Will continue to be,
Since observed by
      Yours faithfully,
          God.

FREE-WILL AND PREDESTINATION

T H E R E was a young man who said " Damn !
It appears to me now that I am
  Just a being that moves
  In predestinate grooves—
Not a bus, not a bus, but a tram."   *Anonymous.*

"The living creature after his kind."

Genesis I. 24.

THE BEASTS

I THINK I could turn and live with animals, they are so
    placid and self-contain'd;
I stand and look at them long and long.
They do not sweat and whine about their condition;
They do not lie awake in the dark and weep for their sins;
They do not make me sick discussing their duty to God;
Not one is dissatisfied—not one is demented with the
    mania of owning things;
Not one kneels to another, nor to his kind that lived
    thousands of years ago;
Not one is respectable or industrious over the whole earth.

Walt Whitman.

FOUR BEASTS

THERE be four things which are little upon the earth
But they are exceeding wise;
The ants are a people not strong,
Yet they prepare their meat in the summer;
The conies are but a feeble folk,
Yet they make their houses in the rocks;
The locusts have no king,
Yet they go forth all of them by bands;
The spider taketh hold with her hands,
And is in kings' palaces.

Authorised Version.

JONAH AND THE WHALE

HE sported round the watery world.
His rich oil was a gloomy waveless lake
Within the waves.   Affrighted seamen hurled
    Their weapons in his foaming wake.

G

One old corroding iron he bore
Which journeyed through his flesh but yet had not
Found out his life.   Another lance he wore
Outside him pricking in a tender spot.

So distant were his parts that they
Sent but a dull faint message to his brain.
He knew not his own flesh, as great kings may
Not know the farther places where they reign.

His play made storm in a calm sea ;
His very kindness slew what he might touch ;
And wrecks lay scattered on his anger's lee.
The Moon rocked to and fro his watery couch.

His hunger cleared the sea.   And where
He passed, the ocean's edge lifted its brim.
He skimmed the dim sea-floor to find if there
Some garden had its harvest ripe for him.

But in his sluggish brain no thought
Ever arose.   His law was instinct blind.
No thought or gleam or vision ever brought
Light to the dark of his old dreamless mind

Until one day sudden and strange
Half-hints of knowledge burst upon his sight.
Glimpses he had of Time, and Space, and Change,
And something greater than his might ;

And terror's leap to imagine sin ;
And blinding Truth half-bare unto his seeing.
It was the living man who had come in . . .
Jonah's thoughts flying through his being.

Viola Meynell.

Fish
HEAVEN

FISH (fly-replete, in depth of June
Dawdling away their wat'ry noon)
Ponder deep wisdom, dark or clear,
Each secret fishy hope or fear.
Fish say, they have their Stream and Pond ;

THE ZOO

But is there anything Beyond?
This life cannot be All, they swear,
For how unpleasant, if it were!
One may not doubt that, somehow, good
Shall come of Water and of Mud;
And, sure, the reverent eye must see
A Purpose in Liquidity.
We darkly know, by Faith we cry,
The future is not Wholly Dry.
Mud unto Mud!—Death eddies near—
Not here the appointed End, not here!
But somewhere, beyond Space and Time,
Is wetter water, slimier slime!
And there (they trust) there swimmeth One
Who swam ere rivers were begun,
Immense, of fishy form and mind,
Squamous, omnipotent, and kind;
And under that Almighty Fin
The littlest fish may enter in.
Oh! never fly conceals a hook,
Fish say, in the Eternal Brook,
But more than mundane weeds are there,
And mud, celestially fair;
Fat caterpillars drift around,
And Paradisal grubs are found;
Unfading moths, immortal flies,
And the worm that never dies.
And in that Heaven of all their wish,
There shall be no more land, say fish.

Rupert Brooke.

THE TYGER

TYGER! tyger! burning bright
In the forests of the night,
What immortal hand or eye
Could frame thy fearful symmetry?

In what distant deeps or skies
Burnt the fire of thine eyes?
On what wings dare he aspire?
What the hand dare seize the fire?

163

And what shoulder and what art
Could twist the sinews of thy heart ?
And, when thy heart began to beat,
What dread hand and what dread feet ?

What the hammer ? what the chain ?
In what furnace was thy brain ?
What the anvil ? what dread grasp
Dare its deadly terrors clasp ?

When the stars threw down their spears,
And water'd heaven with their tears,
Did he smile his work to see ?
Did he who made the lamb make thee ?

Tyger ! tyger ! burning bright
In the forests of the night,
What immortal hand or eye
Dare frame thy fearful symmetry ?

William Blake.

MILK FOR THE CAT

WHEN the tea is brought at five o'clock,
And all the neat curtains are drawn with care,
The little black cat with bright green eyes
Is suddenly purring there.

At first she pretends, having nothing to do,
She has come in merely to blink by the grate,
But, though tea may be late or the milk may be sour,
She is never late.

And presently her agate eyes
Take a soft large, milky haze
And her independent casual glance
Becomes a stiff, hard gaze.

Then she stamps her claws or lifts her ears,
Or twists her tail and begins to stir,
Till suddenly all her lithe body becomes
One breathing, trembling purr.

164

THE ZOO

The children eat and wriggle and laugh,
The two old ladies stroke their silk :
But the cat is grown small and thin with desire,
Transformed to a creeping lust for milk.

The white saucer like some full moon descends
At last from the clouds of the table above ;
She sighs and dreams and thrills and glows,
Transfigured with love.

She nestles over the shining rim,
Buries her chin in the creamy sea ;
Her tail hangs loose ; each drowsy paw
Is doubled under each bending knee.

A long, dim ecstasy holds her life ;
Her world is an infinite shapeless white,
Till her tongue has curled the last holy drop,
Then she sinks back into the night,

Draws and dips her body to heap
Her sleepy nerves in the great arm-chair,
Lies defeated and buried deep
Three or four hours unconscious there.

Harold Monro.

Dog
THE SONG OF QUOODLE

THEY haven't got no noses,
The fallen sons of Eve ;
Even the smell of roses
Is not what they supposes ;
But more than mind discloses
And more than men believe.

They haven't got no noses,
They cannot even tell
When door and darkness closes
The park a Jew encloses,
Where even the Law of Moses
Will let you steal a smell.

THE ZOO

The brilliant smell of water,
The brave smell of a stone,
The smell of dew and thunder,
The old bones buried under,
Are things in which they blunder
And err, if left alone.

The wind from winter forests,
The scent of scentless flowers,
The breath of brides' adorning,
The smell of snare and warning,
The smell of Sunday morning,
God gave to us for ours.

. . . . . .

And Quoodle here discloses
All things that Quoodle can,
They haven't got no noses,
They haven't got no noses,
And goodness only knowses
The Noselessness of Man.

G. K. Chesterton.

THE COW

THE friendly cow all red and white,
   I love with all my heart :
She gives me cream with all her might,
   To eat with apple-tart.

She wanders lowing here and there,
   And yet she cannot stray,
All in the pleasant open air,
   The pleasant light of day ;

And blown by all the winds that pass
   And wet with all the showers,
She walks among the meadow grass
   And eats the meadow flowers.

R. L. Stevenson.

Cow

THE LILY-POOL

W H A T sees our mailie in the lily-pool,
　　What sees she with that large surprise ?
What sees our mailie in the lily-pool
　　With all the violet of her big eyes—
　　　　Our mailie in the lily-pool ?

She sees herself within the lily-pool,
　　Herself in flakes of brown and white—
Herself beneath the slab that is the lily-pool,
　　The green and liquid slab of light
　　　　With cups of silver dight,
　　　　Stem-rooted in the depths of amber night
That hold the hollows of the lily-pool—
　　　　Our own dear lily-pool !

And does she gaze into the lily-pool
　　As one that is enchanted ?
Or does she try the cause to find
　　How the reflection's slanted,
That sleeps within the lily-pool ?
　　Or does she take it all for granted
With the sweet natural logic of her kind ?
　　　　The lazy logic of the lily-pool,
　　　　Our own bright, innocent, stupid lily-pool !

She knows that it is nice—our lily-pool :
　　She likes the water-rings around her knees ;
　　She likes the shadow of the trees,
That droop above the lily-pool ;
　　She likes to scatter with a silly sneeze
The long-legged flies that skim the lily-pool—
The peaceful-sleeping, baby lily-pool.

So may I look upon the lily-pool,
　　Nor ever in the slightest care
　　Why I am there ;
Why upon land and sea
Is ever stamped the inevitable me ;

167

But rather say with that most gentle fool—
" How pleasant is this lily-pool !
How nice and cool !
Be off, you long-legged flies !   O what a spree !
To drive the flies from off the lily-pool !
From off this most sufficient, absolute lily-pool ! "

T. E. Brown.

EPITAPH ON A HARE

H E R E lies, whom hound did ne'er pursue,
   Nor swifter greyhound follow,
Whose foot ne'er tainted morning dew,
   Nor ear heard huntsman's hollo ;

Old Tiney, surliest of his kind,
   Who, nursed with tender care,
And to domestic bounds confined,
   Was still a wild Jack-hare.

Though duly from my hand he took
   His pittance every night,
He did it with a jealous look,
   And when he could, would bite.

His diet was of wheaten bread,
   And milk, and oats, and straw,
Thistles, or lettuces instead,
   With sand to scour his maw.

On twigs of hawthorn he regaled,
   On pippins' russet peel ;
And, when his juicy salads fail'd,
   Sliced carrot pleased him well.

A Turkey carpet was his lawn,
   Whereon he loved to bound,
To skip and gambol like a fawn,
   And swing his rump around.

His frisking was at evening hours,
　　For then he lost his fear;
But most before approaching showers,
　　Or when a storm drew near.

Eight years and five round-rolling moons
　　He thus saw steal away,
Dozing out all his idle noons,
　　And every night at play.

I kept him for his humour's sake,
　　For he would oft beguile
My heart of thoughts that made it ache,
　　And force me to a smile.

But now, beneath this walnut-shade
　　He finds his long last home,
And waits, in snug concealment laid,
　　Till gentler Puss shall come.

He, still more aged, feels the shocks
　　From which no care can save,
And, partner once of Tiney's box,
　　Must soon partake his grave.

William Cowper.

TO A MOUSE, ON TURNING HER UP IN HER NEST WITH THE PLOUGH, NOVEMBER, 1785

WEE, sleekit, cow'rin', tim'rous beastie,
O what a panic's in thy breastie!
Thou need na start awa sae hasty,
　　　　　　Wi' bickering brattle!
I wad be laith to rin an' chase thee
　　　　　　Wi' murd'ring pattle!

I'm truly sorry man's dominion
Has broken Nature's social union,
An' justifies that ill opinion
　　　　　　Which makes thee startle
At me, thy poor earth-born companion,
　　　　　　An' fellow-mortal!

I doubt na, whiles, but thou may thieve;
What then? poor beastie, thou maun live!
A daimen-icker in a thrave
      'S a sma' request:
I'll get a blessin' wi' the lave,
      And never miss 't!

Thy wee bit housie, too, in ruin!
Its silly wa's the win's are strewin'!
An' naething, now, to big a new ane,
      O' foggage green!
An' bleak December's winds ensuin',
      Baith snell an' keen!

Thou saw the fields laid bare and waste,
An' weary winter comin' fast,
An' cozie here, beneath the blast,
      Thou thought to dwell,
Till crash! the cruel coulter past
      Out-thro' thy cell.

That wee bit heap o' leaves an' stibble
Has cost thee mony a weary nibble!
Now thou's turn'd out, for a' thy trouble,
      But house or hald,
To thole the winter's sleety dribble,
      An' cranreuch cauld!

But, Mousie, thou art no thy lane,
In proving foresight may be vain:
The best laid schemes o' mice an' men
      Gang aft a-gley,
An' lea'e us nought but grief an' pain
      For promis'd joy.

Still thou art blest compar'd wi' me!
The present only toucheth thee:
But oh! I backward cast my e'e
      On prospects drear!
An' forward tho' I canna see,
      I guess an' fear!

Robert Burns.

THE ZOO
THE RABBIT

T H E rabbit has a charming face :
Its private life is a disgrace.
I really dare not name to you
The awful things that rabbits do ;
Things that your paper never prints—
You only mention them in hints.
They have such lost, degraded souls
No wonder they inhabit holes ;
When such depravity is found
It only can live underground.

Anon. : 20th Cent.

THE HORSE

I K N O W two things about the horse
And one of them is rather coarse.

Anon. : 20th Cent.

THE KINGFISHER

I T was the Rainbow gave thee birth,
    And left thee all her lovely hues ;
And, as her mother's name was Tears,
    So runs it in thy blood to choose
For haunts the lonely pools, and keep
In company with trees that weep.

Go you and, with such glorious hues,
    Live with proud Peacocks in green parks ;
On lawns as smooth as shining glass,
    Let every feather show its marks ;
Get thee on boughs and clap thy wings
Before the windows of proud kings.

Nay, lovely Bird, thou art not vain ;
    Thou hast no proud ambitious mind ;
I also love a quiet place
    That's green, away from all mankind ;
A lonely pool, and let a tree
Sigh with her bosom over me.   *W. H. Davies.*

THE ZOO
JENNY WREN

HER sight is short, she comes quite near;
A foot to me's a mile to her;
And she is known as Jenny Wren,
The smallest bird in England.   When
I heard that little bird at first,
Methought her frame would surely burst
With earnest song.   Oft had I seen
Her running under leaves so green,
Or in the grass when fresh and wet,
As though her wings she would forget.
And, seeing this, I said to her—
" My pretty runner, you prefer
To be a thing to run unheard
Through leaves and grass, and not a bird ! "
'Twas then she burst, to prove me wrong,
Into a sudden storm of song;
So very loud and earnest, I
Feared she would break her heart and die.
" Nay, nay," I laughed, " be you no thing
To run unheard, sweet scold, but sing !
O I could hear your voice near me,
Above the din in that oak tree,
When almost all the twigs on top
Had starlings chattering without stop."

W. H. Davies.

Blackbird
VESPERS

O BLACKBIRD, what a boy you are !
How you do go it !
Blowing your bugle to that one sweet star—
How you do blow it !
And does she hear you, blackbird boy, so far ?
Or is it wasted breath ?
"Good Lord ! she is so bright
To-night ! "
The blackbird saith

T. E. Brown.

THE OCTOBER REDBREAST

AUTUMN is weary, halt, and old;
  Ah, but she owns the song of joy!
Her colours fade, her woods are cold.
  Her singing-bird's a boy, a boy.

In lovely Spring the birds were bent
  On nests, on use, on love, forsooth!
Grown-up were they. This boy's content,
  For his is liberty, his is youth.

The musical stripling sings for play
  Taking no thought, and virgin-glad.
For duty sang those mates in May.
  This singing-bird's a lad, a lad.

Alice Meynell.

THE EAGLE

HE clasps the crag with crooked hands;
  Close to the sun in lonely lands,
Ringed with the azure world, he stands.

The wrinkled sea beneath him crawls;
He watches from his mountain walls,
And like a thunderbolt he falls.

Alfred Tennyson.

THE GRASSHOPPER

O THOU that swing'st upon the waving hair
  Of some well-fillèd oaten beard,
Drunk every night with a delicious tear
  Dropt thee from Heaven, where thou wert rear'd!

The joys of earth and air are thine entire,
  That with thy feet and wings dost hop and fly;
And when thy poppy works, thou dost retire
  To thy carved acorn-bed to lie.

Up with the day, the Sun thou welcom'st then,
  Sport'st in the gilt plaits of his beams.
And all these merry days mak'st merry men,
  Thyself, and melancholy streams.

Richard Lovelace.

173

THE ANT

FORBEAR, thou great good husband, little ant;
  A little respite from thy flood of sweat !
Thou, thine own horse and cart under this plant,
  Thy spacious tent, fan thy prodigious heat ;
Down with thy double load of that one grain !
It is a granarie for all thy train.

Cease, large example of wise thrift, awhile
  (For thy example is become our law),
And teach thy frowns a seasonable smile :
  So Cato sometimes the nak'd Florals saw,
And thou, almighty foe, lay by thy sting,
Whilst thy unpay'd musicians, crickets, sing.

Lucasta, she that holy makes the day,
  And 'stills new life in fields of feuillemort,
Hath back restor'd their verdure with one ray,
  And with her eye bid all to play and sport,
Ant, to work still ! age will thee truant call ;
And to save now, th'art worse than prodigal.

Austere and cynick ! not one hour t'allow,
  To lose with pleasure, what thou got'st with pain ;
But drive on sacred festivals thy plow,
  Tearing high-ways with thy ore-chargèd wain ;
Not all thy life-time one poor minute live,
And thy ore-labour'd bulk with mirth relieve ?

Look up then, miserable ant, and spie
  Thy fatal foes, for breaking of their law,
Hov'ring above thee : Madam *Margaret Pie* :
  And her fierce servant, meagre Sir *John Daw* :
Thy self and storehouse now they do store up,
And thy whole harvest too within their crop.

Thus we unthrifty thrive within earth's tomb
  For some more rav'nous and ambitious jaw :
The grain in th' ant's, the ant in the pie's womb,
  The pie in th' hawk's, the hawk i' th' eagle's maw.
So scattering to hoard 'gainst a long day,
Thinking to save all, we cast all away.
                                        Richard Lovelace.

THE ZOO
SONNET TO A MONKEY
O LIVELY, O most charming pug,
Thy graceful air, and heavenly mug;
The beauties of his mind do shine,
And every bit is shaped and fine.
Your teeth are whiter than the snow,
You're a great buck, you're a great beau;
Your eyes are of so nice a shape,
More like a Christian's than an ape;
Your cheek is like the rose's blume,
Your hair is like the raven's plume;
His nose's cast is of the Roman,
He is a very pretty woman.
I could not get a rhyme for Roman,
So was obliged to call him woman.

Marjorie Fleming (obit 1811, *ætat*: 8).

Man
HYMN TO MOLOCH
O THOU who didst furnish
The fowls of the air
With loverly feathers
For leydies to wear,
Receive this Petition
For blessin an aid,
From the principal Ouses
Engaged in the Trade.

The trouble's as follows:
A white livered Scum,
What if they was choked
T'would be better for some,
S'been pokin about an
Creatin a fuss
An talkin too loud to be
Ealthy for us.

Thou'lt ardly believe
Ow damn friendly they are,
They say there's a time
In the future not far

THE ZOO

When birds worth good money'll
Waste by the ton
An the Trade can look perishin
Pleased to look on.

With best lines in Paradies
Equal to what
Is fetchin a pony
A time in the at,
An ospreys an ummins
An other choice goods
Wastefully 'oppin
About in the woods.

They're kiddin the papers,
An callin us names,
Not Yorkshire ones neither,
That's one of their games,
They've others as pleasin
An soakin with spite,
An it don't make us appy,
Ow can it do, quite !

We thank thee most earty
For mercies to date,
The Olesales is pickin
Nice profits per crate,
Reports from the Retails
Is pleasin to read
We certainly thank thee
Most earty indeed.

Vouchsafe, then, to muzzle
These meddlesome swine,
An learn em to andle goods
More in their line,
Be faithful, be foxy
Till peril is past,
An plant thy strong sword
In their livers at last.

Ralph Hodgson.

THE ZOO
MAN AND BEAST

I AM less patient than this horse
And it is fleeter far than I.
Its hair is silky, mine is coarse;
Grasses have shaped that larger eye,
While to feed me live things must die.

The birds make little darts in air,
And fishes little darts in water,
Old sheep a silver glory share,
Peacocks are peacocks everywhere . . .
Man lies awake, planning the slaughter.

What woman has this old cat's graces?
What boy can sing as the thrush sings?
For me, I'd rather not run races
With dragon-flies, nor thread the mazes
Of a smooth lawn with ants and things.

Yet horse and sheep tread leaf and stem
And bud and flower beneath their feet;
They sniff at Stars-of-Bethlehem
And buttercups are food to them—
No more than bitter food or sweet.

I, to whom air and waves are sealed,
I yet possess the human part.
O better beasts, you now must yield!
I name the cool stars of the field,
I have the flowers of heaven by heart.

Francis Meynell.

" Everyone suddenly burst out singing."
Siegfried Sassoon.

GREEN GROW THE RASHES, O!

With point and not too quickly.

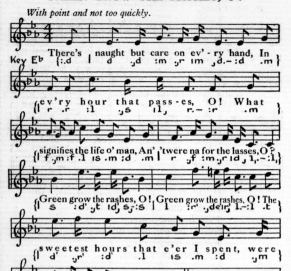

Key Eb

There's naught but care on ev'-ry hand, In

ev'ry hour that pass-es, O! What

signifies the life o' man, An' 'twere na for the lasses, O?

Green grow the rashes, O! Green grow the rashes, O! The

sweetest hours that e'er I spent, were

spent among the lasses, O! *Repeat from the double bar for chorus.*

Gie me a cannie hour at e'en,
My arms about my dearie, O!
An warldly cares and warldly men,
May a' gae tapsalteerie, O!

For you sae douce wha sneer at this,
Ye're nought but senseless asses, O!
The wisest man the warld e'er saw,
He dearly lo'ed the lasses, O!

Auld nature swears the lovely dears,
Her noblest work she classes, O!
Her 'prentice han' she tried on man,
An' then she made the lasses, O!

Robert Burns.

181

ONE MORE RIVER

In march time.

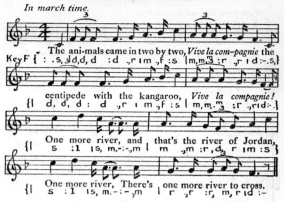

The ani-mals came in two by two, *Vive la com-pagnie* the

Key F { : .s ,s|d,d, d : d ,r ı m ,f :s |m,m.m̲₃ :r ,r ı d :-.s,}

centipede with the kangaroo, *Vive la compagnie!*

{| d, d, d : d ,r ı m ,f :s |m,m.m̲₃ :r ,r ı d :-.}

One more river, and that's the river of Jordan,

{| s :1 ıs, m.-:-,m | m ,m :r ,d₂ ,r ı m :s }

One more river, There's one more river to cross.

{| s :1 1s, m.-:-,m | r ,r :r, m ,r ı d :- }

The animals came in three by three,
  Vive la compagnie.
The elephant on the back of the flea,
  Vive la compagnie.
   One more river, etc.

The animals came in four by four, etc.

The camel, he got stuck in the door.

Some were dead and some were alive.

The monkey he was up to his tricks.

Some went to Hell, and some went to Heaven.

The worm was early, the bird was late.

Some had water and some had wine.

If you want any more you must sing it again.

BILLY BOY

Loud and with good rhythm.

Where have ye been all the day, Bil - ly Boy,

Key E {l m:—:f │ s:—:s │ f:—:m│r:—:l │ m:—:r │d:—:}

Bil-ly Boy? Where have ye been all the day, me

{l r:—:t │ d:—:l │ m:—:f │ s:—:s │ f:—:s│l:—:s }

Bil — ly Boy . . . I've been walk-ing all the

{l fe:—:s │ r:—:l:—:l:—:s:—:s │ l:—:s │l:—:t }

day . . with me charming Nan - cy Grey and me

{l d:—:t │l:—:s │ l:—:s │f:—:m:r │ d:—:t, l,:—:s, }

Nancy kittled me fancy, Oh, me charming Billy Boy!

{l d:d:d│m:r:d│ s:—:s│l:—:d │ m:—:d │r:—:t│d:—:}

Can she cook a bit o' steak, Billy Boy, Billy Boy?
Can she cook a bit o' steak, me Billy Boy?
    She can cook a bit o' steak,
    Aye, and make a girdle cake.
       And me Nancy, etc.

Is she fit to be your wife, Billy Boy, Billy Boy?
Is she fit to be your wife, me Billy Boy?
    She's as fit to be me wife
    As the fork is to the knife.
       And me Nancy, etc.

Did she lie close unto thee, Billy Boy, Billy Boy?
Did she lie close unto thee, Billy Boy?
    Yes, she lay close unto me
    As the bark is to the tree,
       And me Nancy, etc.

183

THE MALLARD

Bucolically and fairly fast.

Key G. {:s | d :t, :d (ate) :l, | r :de :r it, :— :t, .t, }
O I have a-yut, O what have I yut? I've a-

{ l m :—:m ls, :s, :s, l s, :d :— :—: : l s, :l, :t, ld :—: }
yut the toe o' my mallard. 'Tis a toe-toe,

{ l d :t :l ls: :s l d :d :d ld :r :m }
nip-pens and all. O I have a-yut o' my

{ l s, :m :d il,: :l, l r :r :r is,:— :s, }
mal-lard-y O, So good-um it was, my

{ l s, :d :— : :s l d :t, :d :d il,: — :l, }
mallard. 2. O I have a-yut, O

{ l r :de :r it :— :t, .t, l m:—:m (foot) s, :s, l s :d :—: : }
what have I yut? I've a-yut the voot o' my mallard,

{ l d :d :d ld :d id :d :t :l id :t :l ls: :s }
a voot-voot, a toe-toe, nippens and all, O

{ l d :d :d id :r :m l s :m :d il,: :l, }
I have a yut o' my mal-lard-y O, So

{ l r :r :r is,:—:s l s :d :—: :ll }
good-um it was, my mallard.

*Repeat this half bar so as to take in a fresh addition with every verse, for instance " a thigh-thigh, a leg-leg, a voot-voot, a toe-toe, *nippens and all*," etc. The order is : (1) Toe ; (2) Voot ; (3) Leg ; (4) Thigh ; (5) Hip ; (6) Rump ; (7) Zide ; (8) Wing ; (9) Back, etc.

184

BUNYAN'S HYMN

(From the English Hymnal)

Fairly quickly and with fervour.

He who would valiant be 'gainst all dis-as-ter

Let — him in con-stan-cy, fol-

low the Mas-ter. There's no discourage-

ment shall make him once re-lent, His

first avowed in-tent to be a pilgrim.

Who so beset him round
    With dismal stories,
Do but themselves confound—
    His strength the more is.
No foes shall stay his might,
    Though he with giant's fight :
He will make good his right
    To be a pilgrim.

Since, Lord, thou dost defend
    Us with Thy Spirit,
We know we at the end
    Shall life inherit.
Then fancies flee away !
    I'll fear not what men say,
I'll labour night and day
    To be a pilgrim.

EN PASSANT PAR LA LORRAINE

At a good swinging pace.

En pas - sant par la Lor - raine, A - vec mes sa -
Key F |d:-:d | s:-:s | s:-:s | l:-:f | s:-:s | l:-:l

(Chorus.)

bots, En pas - sant par la Lor - rain - e A - vec
|s:-:-l-:-:|d:-:d | s:-:s | s:-:s | l:-:f | s:-:s

(Solo.)

mes sa - bots, Ren - con - trai trois cap - i -
|l:-:l | s:-:-l-: : | s:-:s | d':-:s | s:-:f

tain - es, A - vec mes sabots, Don - dain - e
| m:-:r | m:-:m | m:-:s | s:-:f | m:-:r

Oh! Oh! Oh! A - vec mes sa - bots.
|d:-:m | s:-l-: : | l:-:f | r:-:t, | d,:-:l-: : :

(Chorus.)

Ren - con - trai trois ca - pi - tai - nes, Av - vec
|s:-:s | d:-:s | s:-:f | m:-:r | m:-:m

mes sa - bots, Don - dai - ne, Oh! Oh! Oh!
|m:-:s | s:-:f | m:-:r |d:-:m | s:-:l-: :

A - vec mes sa - bots.
|l:-:f | r:-:t | d:-:-l-:-:||

186

Rencontrai trois capitaines, Avec mes sabots,
(repeat chorus).

Ils m'ont appelé vilaine, Avec mes sabots,
  Dondaine, Oh! Oh! Oh! Avec mes sabots.
(Repeat chorus).

Ils m'ont appelé vilaine, Avec mes sabots,
Je ne suis pas si vilaine, Avec, etc.

Je ne suis pas si vilaine, etc.
Puisque le fils du roi m'aime, etc.

Puisque le fils du roi m'aime,
Il m'a donné pour étrenne.

Il m'a donné pour étrenne,
Un bouquet de marjolaine.

Un bouquet de marjolaine,
S'il fleurit, je serai reine.

S'il fleurit, je serai reine,
S'il y meurt je perds ma peine.

MR. REILLY

AUPRÈS DE MA BLONDE

In march time.

Dans les jardins d'mon pè—re Les li-las sont fleu-ris,——— Dans les jardins d'mon pè-re Les li-las sont fleu-ris——— Tous les oi-seaux du mon-de Vien'nt y faire leurs nids — Au-près de ma blon-de, Qu'il fait bon, fait bon, fait bon, Au—près de ma blon-de, Qu'il fait bon dor—

Tous les oiseaux du monde } Repeat.
Vien'nt y faire leurs nids

La caill', la tourterelle
Et la joli' perdrix—Auprès de ma blonde, etc.

N.B—The two new lines in each verse are sung twice at the beginning of the following verse.

La caill', etc., etc.
Et ma joli' colombe
Qui chante jour et nuit.

Qui chante pour les filles
Qui n'ont pas de mari.

Pour moi ne chante guère
Car j'en ai un joli.

Dites-nous donc la belle,
Ou donc est votr' mari.

Il est dans la Hollande
Les Hollandais l'ont pris.

Que donneriez-vous belle,
Pour avoir votre ami ?

Je donnerais Versailles,
Paris et Saint Denis.

Les tours de Notre Dame,
Et l'clocher d'mon pays.

Et ma joli' colombe,
Pour avoir mon mari.

THEY WERE ONLY PLAYING LEAP-FROG

Quick march time.

They were on-ly play-ing leap-frog.

They were on-ly play-ing leap-frog.

They were on-ly play-ing leap-frog, When one grass-hop-per jumped up-on the other gras-hop-per's back.

BOBBY SHAFTOE

Fairly quickly.
(Chorus.)

Key A

1. {Bobby Shaftoe's gone to sea, Silver buckles
| d .d :d .f | m .s :m .d | s .s, :s, .d |

{on his knee ; He'll come back and marry me,—
| t .t, :r .t, .s, | d .t, :d .f | m .s :m .d |

(Verse.)
Bonny Bobby Shaf - toe. Bobby Shaftoe's
| r .f :r .t, | d :d ‖ m .s :m .d

{bright and fair, Combing down his yellow hair;
| m .s :m | r .f :r .t, | r .f :r

(Repeat Chorus.)
{He's my ain for ever mair, Bonny Bobby Shaf-toe.
| m .s :m .d | m .s :m | r .f :r .t, | d :d ‖

Bobby Shaftoe 's tall and slim,
He's always dressed so neat and trim,
The lassies they all keek at him,
Bonny Bobby Shaftoe.
    Chorus.

Bobby Shaftoe's gett'n a bairn,
For to dangle on his airm,
On his airm and on his knee,
Bonny Bobby Shaftoe,

Final Chorus :
    Bobby Shaftoe's been to sea,
    Silver buckles on his knee,
    He's come back and married me,
    Bonny Bobby Shaftoe.
(And so on, *ad infinitum,* getting faster and faster.)

THE BARLEY MOW

With inebriation.

Here's a health to the Bar-ley Mow, my boys, A
health to the Bar-ley Mow. (1) We'll
drink it out of a nut-brown bowl, A
health to the Bar-ley Mow. The nip-perkin, pipperkin
and the brown bowl, A health to the Bar-ley

Repeat to the double bar.

Mow, my boys, A health to the Barley Mow.

We'll drink it out of the pint, my boys,

We'll drink it out of the gallon, my boys,

We'll drink it out of the river, my boys,

We'll drink it out of the ocean, my boys,

MASSA'S IN DE COLD, COLD GROUND

Slowly and sadly.

Key D♭

Round de meadows am a-ring--ing de
darkey's mourn-ful song, While de mocking bird am
sing-ing Happy as de day am long.
Where de ivy am a-creep-ing O'er de gras-sy
mound, Dere de massa am a-sleep---ing,
sleeping in de cold, cold ground. Down in de
corn-field Hear dat mournful sound;
All de darkey's am a-weep-ing Massa's in de cold, cold
ground.

When de Autumn leaves are falling,
    When de days were cold,
'Twas hard to hear old Massa calling,
    Cayse he was so weak and old.

Now de orange tree am blooming
  On de sandy shore,
Now de summer days are coming
  Massa nebber calls no more.
    Down, etc.

Massa makes de darkeys love him,
  Cayse he was so kind,
Now dey sadly weep above him,
  Mourning cayse he leave dem behind.
I cannot work before to-morrow,
  Cayse de tear-drop flow,
I try to drive away my sorrow,
  Picking on de old banjo.
    Down, etc.

GOLDEN SLUMBERS KISS YOUR EYES

Quietly and rather slowly.

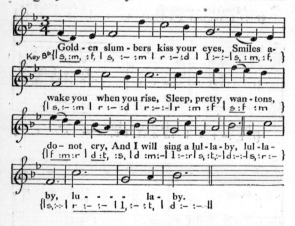

Care is heavy, therefore sleep,
  You are care, and care must keep,
  Sleep, pretty wantons, etc.

AND WHEN I DIE

Slowly and with much pathos.

feet,

{| l, :- | : | And then I know | d :t :le | t. :- | : |}

at my head and my feet

{| :f .f|m :r :r | l, :- | : | :s |f :r}

my bones will keep

{| :s, |l, :t, | d :-:-:- |}

know my bones will keep

{| t, :s |fe :f | m :-:- ||}

FRÈRE JACQUES

Not slowly.   (*Round for four voices.*)

1.   4.

Fre - re   Jac - ques,   Fre - re   Jac - ques

Key G {| d :r |m :d | d :r |m :d ||}

2.   3.

Dor - mez   vous?   Dor - mez   vous?

{| m :f | s :- | m :f | s :- ||}

3.   2.

Sonnez les ma - tin - es, Sonnez les ma - tin - es

{| s ,|s .f |m :d | s ,|s .f |m :d ||}

4.   1.

Dig, din, don.   Dig, din, don.

{| d :s, | d :- | d :s, | d :- ||}

HE THAT WILL AN ALE-HOUSE KEEP

Not too quickly. (*Round for three voices.*)

COME, LANDLORD, FILL THE FLOWING BOWL

Bibulously.

The man who drinketh small beer,
  And goes to bed quite sober,
Fades as the leaves do fade,
  That drop off in October.
    For to-night, etc.

The man who drinketh strong beer,
  And goes to bed quite mellow,
Lives as he aught to live,
  And dies a jolly good fellow.
    For to-night, etc.

But he who drinks just what he likes
  And getteth half-seas over,
Will live until he dies perhaps,
  And then lie down in clover.
    For to-night, etc.

The man who kisses a pretty girl,
  And goes and tells his mother,
Ought to have his lips cut off,
  And never kiss another.
    For to-night, etc.

ROUND THE CORNER

Roisterously and in march time.

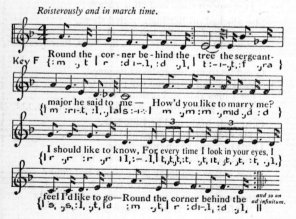

Round the cor-ner be-hind the tree the sergeant-

Key F {:m ,t |r :d-.l,:d ,|l, t:-l,t:f ,:a}

major he said to me — How'd you like to marry me?

{|m :r:-t, :l, ,|a|s:-:-| m ,:m:m ,:m|d ,d :d }

I should like to know, For every time I look in your eyes, I

{|r ,:r :r ,:r ,|l,:-.l| t,:t,t,:t, ,:t,|t, ,:t, :t, ,:l,}

feel I'd like to go—Round the corner behind the

{|s, ,:s, :l, ,:t,|d :m ,t| r :d:-.l,:d ,:|l, ||

*and so on
ad infinitum.*

THE WRAGGLE TAGGLE GIPSIES, O!

Not slowly.

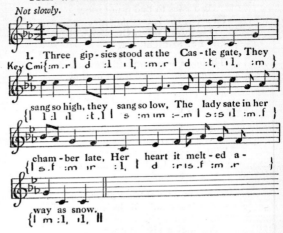

1. Three gip-sies stood at the Cas-tle gate, They

Key Cmi {:m .r | d :l ıl, :m .r | d :t, ıl, :m }

sang so high, they sang so low, The lady sate in her

{| l :l ıl :t .l | s :m ım :–.m | s :s ıl :m .f }

cham-ber late, Her heart it melt-ed a-

{| s .f :m ır :l, | d :r ıs .f :m .r }

way as snow.

{| m :l, ıl, ‖ }

They sang so sweet, they sang so shrill,
   That fast her tears began to flow.
And she laid down her silken gown,
   Her golden rings and all her show.

She plucked off her high-heeled shoes,
   A-made of Spanish leather, O
She would in the street, with her bare, bare feet ;
   All out in the wind and weather, O.

O saddle to me my milk-white steed,
   And go and fetch me my pony, O !
That I may ride and seek my bride,
   Who is gone with the wraggle taggle gipsies, O !

O he rode high, and he rode low,
   He rode through wood and copses too,
Until he came to an open field,
   And there he espied his a-lady, O !

What makes you leave your house and land ?
   Your golden treasures for to go ?
What makes you leave your new-wedded lord,
   To follow the wraggle taggle gipsies, O ?

What care I for my house and my land?
 What care I for my treasure, O?
What care I for my new-wedded lord,
 I'm off with the wraggle taggle gipsies, O!

Last night you slept on a goose-feather bed,
 With the sheet turned down so bravely, O!
And to-night you'll sleep in a cold open field,
 Along with the wraggle taggle gipsies, O!

What care I for a goose-feather bed,
 With the sheet turned down so bravely, O!
For to-night I shall sleep in a cold open field,
 Along with the wraggle taggle gipsies, O!

MR. McKINLEY

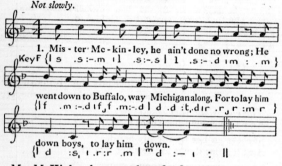

Mr. McKinley, he went there for fun,
But Sholgosh he shot him with an Ivor-Johnson gun,
For to lay him down boys, to lay him down.

Mrs. McKinley, she hollered and she swore
When they told her her good man wasn't coming home
 no more,
For to lay him down boys, to lay him down.

Sholgosh, they took him and put him in the electric chair,
And shocked him so hard that they shocked off all his
 hair,
For to lay him down boys, to lay him down.

199

BINNORIE, OR THE CRUEL SISTER

Sadly, but with strength.

There were twa sis-ters sat in a bower, Bin-
nor-ie, O, Bin-nor-ie; There cam' a knight to
be their wooer, By the bon - ny mill-dams o'- Bin-
nor - - ie.

He courted the eldest wi' glove and ring, Binnorie, etc.
But he lo'ed the youngest, a-boon a thing, By the, etc.

The eldest she was vexed sair,
And sore envied her sister fair.

She's ta'en her by the lily hand,
And led her down to the river strand.

The youngest stude upon a stane,
The eldest cam' and pushed her in.

Sometimes she sank, sometimes she swam,
Until she cam' to the miller's dam.

The miller's daughter was baking bread,
And gaed for water as she had need.

Oh, father, father, draw your dam,
There's either a mermaid or a milk-white swan.

The miller hasted and drew his dam,
And there he found a drowned woman.

A famous harper passing by,
The sweet pale face he chanced to spy.

200

He made a harp o' her breast bone,
Whose sounds would melt a heart of stone.

The strings he framed of her yellow hair,
Their notes made sad the listener.

He brought it to her father's ha'
There was the court assembled a'.

He laid the harp upon a stane,
And straight it began to play alane.

" O' yonder sits my father the king,
And yonder sits my mother, the queen."

" And yonder sits my brother Hugh,
And by him my William, sweet and true."

But the last time that the harp did play,
Was, " woe to my sister, false Helen."

ADAM BUCKHAM, O !

March time.

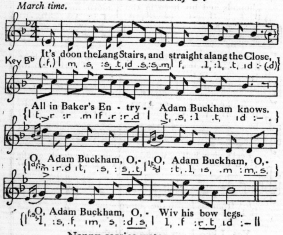

Nanny carries water,
Tommy cobbles shoes,
And Adam gans about,
Geth'ring in the news.
O Adam Buckham, etc.

JOHN PEEL

With vigour.

Key E♭ {:m.m | s :s | m :m .m | s :s | m :m.m }
1. D'ye ken John Peel with his coat so gay, D'ye

{| f :f | r :r .r | f :f .f | r :r .r }
ken John Peel at the break of the day, D'ye

{| d :d | d' :d' .t | l :l ,l | s :f .m }
ken John Peel when he's far, far away, With his

{| l :f .r | d :t, .t, | r :- | d :m .m }
hounds and his horn in the morn ing? For the

{| s :s .s | m :m | s :s .s | m :m.m }
sound of his horn brought me from my bed, And the

{| f :f .f | r :r | .r | f :f | r : }
cry of his hounds which he oft-times led

{| d :d .,d | d :d' .t | l :l ,l | s :f .m }
Peel's view hall'oo would a — waken the dead, or the

{| l :f .r | d :t, .t, | r :- | d : ‖ }
fox from his lair in the morn-ing.

Yes, I ken John Peel and Ruby too !
Ranter and Ringwood, Bellman and True,
From a find to a check, from a check to a view,
From a view to a death in the morning.
     For the sound, etc.

Then here's to John Peel from my heart and soul,
Let's drink to his health, let's finish the bowl,
We'll follow John Peel thro' fair and thro' foul,
If we want a good hunt in the morning
    For the sound, etc.

D'ye ken John Peel with his coat so gay?
He lived at Troutbeck once on a day;
Now he has gone far, far away;
We shall ne'er hear his voice in the morning.
    For the sound, etc.

SWING LOW, SWEET CHARIOT

Intensely and rather slowly.

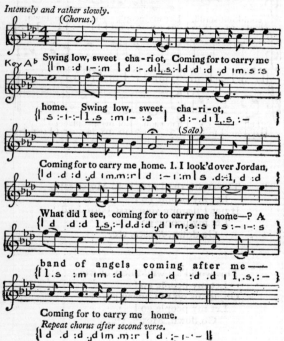

Repeat chorus after second verse.

GO DOWN, MOSES

Boldly. Not too fast.

When Is - rael was in E - gypt's lan',
Key Ami {:m | d' :d' | t :t | d' :d' | l :- }

Let my people go, Op - press'd so hard they
{|m :m |se.se:l| l :-:-:m | d' :d' | t :t }

could not stand, Let my people go! Go down,
{| d' :d | l :- | m :m |se.se:l| l :-:- | l :l :-:- }

Moses, 'Way down in E - gypt's lan'——
{|r' :r'|:-:-| m':- |m':-.r'| m:-.r'| d',l :-:- }

Tell - ole - - Pha - raoh Let my people go!
{|d'.l :l:-:d'| l.s :m:-:| m :m |se.se:l| l:-:-:l }

Thus saith the Lord, bold Moses said,
Let my people go !
If not I'll smite your first-born dead,
Let my people go !
Go down, Moses, etc.

This world's a wilderness of woe,
Let my people go !
Oh, let us on to Canaan go,
Let my people go !
Go down, Moses, etc.

MADEMOISELLE FROM ARMENTIÈRES

In rousing march time.

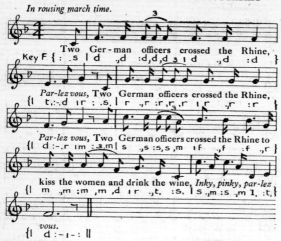

Two Ger-man officers crossed the Rhine,

Key F. {| :s |d .,d :d,d,d₃|d .,d :d |}

Par-lez vous, Two German officers crossed the Rhine,

{|t :,d |r :r .,s.|r .,r :r,r,r |r .,r :r |}

Par-lez vous, Two German officers crossed the Rhine to

{|d :-.r |m :3,m|s .,s :s,s,m |f .,f :f .,r |}

kiss the women and drink the wine, *Inky, pinky, par-lez*

{|m .,m :m .,m,d |r :,t. :s. |s .,m :s .,m |1. :,t.|}

vous.

{| d :-|-: ||}

They came to an inn at the top of the rise,
        Parlez vous,
A famous French inn of enormous size,
        Parlez vous,
    They saw a maiden all dimples and sighs,
    Then both together said, "Damn her eyes."
        Inky pinky, parlez, vous.

Oh, landlord, have you a daughter fair,
        Parlez vous,
Oh, landlord, have you a daughter fair,
        Parlez vous,
    Oh, landlord, have you a daughter fair,
    With lily-white arm, and golden hair?
        Inky pinky, parlez, vous.

N.B.—Other verses may be written on the blank pages at the end of this book.

205

Triumphantly.

I got a robe, you got a robe; All of God's children got a

robe; When I get to Heaven goin' to

put on my robe, goin' to shout all o-ver God's

Heav'n n n   Heav'n n n   Heav'n n n.

(Ev'ry bod-y talkin' 'bout heav'n ain't goin' there!)

Heav'n,   Heav'n—— Goin' to shout all o-ver God's

Heav'n.

I got a shoes, you got a shoes,
All of God's children got a shoes;
When I get to Heav'n goin' to put on my shoes,
Goin' to walk all over God's Heav'n,
    Heav'n, Heav'n . . . etc.

I got a harp, you got a harp,
All of God's children got a harp;
When I get to Heav'n goin' to play on my harp.
Goin' to play all over God's Heav'n,
    Heav'n, Heav'n . . . etc.

206

I got a song, you got a song,
All of God's children got a song ;
When I get to Heav'n goin' to sing a new song,
Going to sing all over God's Heav'n,
    Heav'n, Heav'n . . . etc.

ETON BOYS

With feeling and a nasal Cockney intonation.

With ecstasy and not too slowly.

(harves'

E mi

Sin-ner, please, doan let dis har-ves' pass;
pass)

(harves'

Sin-ner, please, doan let dis har-ves' pass,
pass)

Sin-ner, please, doan let dis har-ves' pass, an'

die an' lose yo' soul at las'.——— 1. I know that

my Re-deem-er lives, (Yes, He lives) I know that

my Re-deem-er lives, (Yes, He lives) I know that

my Re-deem-er lives, Sin-ner, please, doan

let dis har-ves' pass (har-ves' pass).   D.S.

208

My God is a mighty man of war (man of war),
My God is a mighty man of war (man of war),
My God is a mighty man of war,
Sinner, please, doan let dis harves' pass (harves' pass).

I'M A MAN THAT'S DONE WRONG TO MY PARENTS

Sentimentally and with a Cockney accent.

I'm a man that's in trouble and sorrow, That once was light-hearted and gay; Not a coin in this world can I borrow, Since my own I have squandered a-way. I once wronged my father and mother, Till they turned me out from their door —— To beg, starve or die, in the gutter to lie, And ne'er enter their portals no more --- I'm a

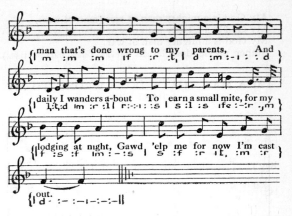

{man that's done wrong to my parents,   And
{ m :m :m |f :r :t, | d :m :-1 : d }

{daily I wanders a-bout   To earn a small mite, for my
{ l, :t :d | m :r :l | r :-:-: :s | s :l :s | fe :-:r ,m }

{lodging at night, Gawd 'elp me for now I'm cast
{ f :s :f | m :- :s | s :f :r |t, :m :r }

{ out.
{ | d : - : :-1-:-:-||

Then my father will say when 'e meets me,
  " You beggar, you still are at large,
And mind, sir, that you don't come near me,
  Or by 'eaven I'll give you in charge."
My mother, poor thing's broken-'earted,
  To meet me she oft-times will try,
For to give me a crown with 'er 'ead 'anging down,
  And a tear rolling out of 'er eye.
        I'm a man, etc.

I've a sister that's married a squire,
  She'll ne'er look, nor speak unto me:
Because in this world she's much 'igher,
  And rides in 'er carriage so free.
And I try to be honest and upright
  And do all the good that I can,
And I try all I know to get on in this world,
  And prove to my friends I'm a man.
        I'm a man, etc.

THE SHAN WAN WOCHT

Quick march time. Very rhythmically.

Key D {Oh - - Boney's on the sea, says the

Shan wan wocht, Oh— Boney's on the sea, says the

Shan wan wocht, Oh— Boney's on the sea, He'll be

here the first o' May, And the

Orange will decay, says the Shan wan wocht, And the

Orange will decay, says the Shan wan wocht

Oh, Boney's on the shore,
   Says the Shan wan wocht, [*twice*
Boney's on the shore,
Don't you hear his cannon's roar?
We'll be Orangemen no more,
   Says the Shan wan wocht.

Oh, Boney's on dry land,
   Says the Shan wan wocht, [*twice*
Oh, Boney's on dry land,
He's a sword in ev'ry hand,
He's a loyal Ribbon man,
   Says the Shan wan wocht.

211

O, ME TATERS !

As you like it.

Key F

O, me ta-ters and me 'ot fried fish ; You can 'ave a little if you wish, You can 'ave it on a plate or on a dish, or in a lit-tle bit o' pa - - - per !

THE LAST LONG MILE

Quick march time.   With a good swing.
(Solo.)

Key Eᵇ

They put us in the Army and they handed us a pack, They took away our nice new clothes and dress'd us up in kak, They marched us twenty miles and more to fit us for the war, We did'nt mind the nineteen but the last one made us sore. (Chorus.) Oh, it's not the pack, that you carry on your back, nor the gun upon your shoulder, Nor the

212

Key E♭ { :f :m | r :s | m ,f :r ,m | d :m }
fiye-inch crust of France's dirty dust That

{ :r ,m | r ,m | r :l | d :t, l, :s, ,s, }
makes you feel your limbs are growing old - er. It's

{ d :.d | t, l, ,s | d :d | t, :s }
not the load on the hard straight road that

{ d :r :m :f | s :-:l | t | d' :t l, :s }
drives a - way your smile; If the sox of sister

{ d :t, l, :s | m ,d :s, ,d | m :r | d :-l:-‖ }
raise a blis - ter, Blame it on the last long mile.

One day we had manœuvres on dear old Salisbury
    Plain,
We marched and marched and marched and marched
    and marched and marched again.
I thought the Duke of York a fool, but he wasn't in
    the van
With us who marched and marched and marched and
    marched back home again.

Chorus.

Oh, it's not the pack, that you carry on your back,
Nor the gun upon your shoulder,
If there's never any ham, there's plum and apple jam
To make you feel your limbs are growing older.
Oh, it's not the camp, nor the echoes of the tramp
That drives away your smile,
It's the sergeant-major's little wager,
To beat you on the last long mile.

213

THE FIRE SHIP

O Sir you must excuse me for being out so late,
For if my parents knew of it, then sad would be my
    fate,
My father he's a minister, a true and honest man,
My mother she's a Methodist, and I do the best I can.
      She'd a dark and a rolling eye, etc.

I took her to a tavern and I treated her to wine,
Little did I think she belonged to the rakish kind;
I handled her, I dandled her, and found to my
surprise,
She was nothing but a fire-ship rigged up in a disguise.
    She'd a dark and a rolling eye, etc.

SHENANDOAH

Slowly, with great longing.

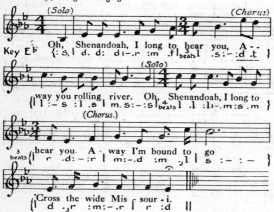

Oh Shenandoah, I love your daughter.
Oh Shenandoah, I love your daughter.

'Tis seven long years since last I see thee.
'Tis seven long years since last I see thee.

Oh Shenandoah, I took a notion
To sail across the stormy ocean.

Oh Shenandoah, I'm bound to leave you.
Oh Shenandoah, I'll not deceive you.

THE EASTER HYMN

("*Unser lieben Frauen Osterfreud*") 1623

With much elation.

Lasst uns er - freu - en herz - lich sehr! Ma - ri - a
Come, let our songs of glad - ness rise! Ma - ry no

{ d :d .r | m .d :m .f | s :- | d :d .r }

seufzt und weint nicht mehr Al - le - lu - ja, Al - le -
lon - ger weeps and sighs, Hal - le - lu - ia, Hal - le -

{ m .d :m .f | s :- | s :d' .t | l :s :d' .t }

lu - ja. Ver - schwun - den a - l - le Ne - bel
lu - ia. For gloom and cloud have passed a-

{ l :s :- | d' d' .s :s .f | :m .f }

sein, Jetzt scheint der lie - be — Son - nen - schein, Al - le
way, Now shines the bless - ed light of day, Hal - le

{ s :d' .l | d' .s :s .f | m .f :s :f .m }

- lu - ja, Al - le - lu - ja, Al - le - lu - ja, Al - le -
- lu - ia, Hal - le - lu - ia, Hal - le - lu - ia, Hal - le -

{ r :d :f .m | r :d :d'.t | l :s :d'.t }

- lu - ja, Al - le - lu - - ja.
- lu - ia, Hal - le - lu - - ia.

{ l :s :f .m | r :- | d :- || }

Aus Seinen Wunden fliessen hier,
Fünf Freuden-See, fünf Freuden-Meer, Alleluja, etc.
Und über dich die Freuden giess,
Dir in dein Herz der Freuden Fluss.

Dein Herz jetzund in Freuden schwimmt,
Je mehr und mehr die Freud' zunimmt,
Ach Frau, vergiss nur unser nicht,
Und teil' uns auch die Freuden mit.

216

See from the wounds of thy dear Son
Five healing streams of gladness run.
The flowing tide thy grief shall still,
Thy heart with floods of gladness fill.

Now thy glad heart with joy o'erflows,
Now more and more thy gladness grows,
O, Mary, keep us in thy care,
And let us all thy gladness share.

MY AUNT

March time.

Repeat from the double bar.

THE TREES THEY DO GROW HIGH

Very sadly and not too fast.

Key G

The trees they do grow high, and the leaves they do grow green, And many a cold winter's night my love and I have seen. Of a cold winters night, my love, you and I a-lone have been, Whilst my bon-ny boy is young; he's a grow-ing.

(Chorus)

Grow-ing, grow-ing whilst my bon-ny lad is young, he's a-grow-ing.

"Oh father, dearest father, you've done to me much
    harm.
You've tied me to a boy when you know he is too young."
"Oh daughter, dearest daughter, if you'll wait a little
A lady you shall be whilst he's growing."   [while,
        Growing, growing, a lady, etc.

"I'll send your love to college all for a year or two,
And then in the meantime he will do for you;

218

I'll buy him white ribbons, tie them round his bonny
To let the ladies know that he's married."   [waist,
      Married, married, to let, etc.

At the age of sixteen he was a married man,
At the age of seventeen he was father to a son,
At the age of eighteen the grass grew over him,
Cruel death soon put an end to his growing,
      Growing, growing, cruel death, etc.

" And now my love is dead, and in his grave doth lie,
The green grass grows over him so very very high,
I'll sit and mourn his fate until the day I die,
And I'll watch all over his child, whilst he's growing,"
      Growing, growing, and I'll, etc.

SONG OF THE HAULERS ON THE VOLGA

MRS. DYER, THE BABY FARMER

Indignantly.

Key G

1. The old baby far-mer 'as been exe-
cu-ted, It's quite time she was put out of the
way. She was a bad wo-man, it is not dis-
put-ed, Not a word in her fa-vour can
an-y-one say.

Chorus.

The old baby farmer, the wretched Mrs. Dyer
   At *the* Old Bailey her wages is paid.
In times long ago we'd ha' made a big fyer
   And roasted so nicely that wicked old jade.

It seems rather hard to run down a woman,
   But this one was hardly a woman at all;
To get a fine livin' in a way so unhuman,
   Crossin' (carousing?) in luxury on poor girls' downfall.
                                    —*Chorus.*

Poor girls who fall from the straight path of virtue,
   What *could* they do with a child in their arms?
The fault they committed they could not undo,
   So the baby was sent to the cruel baby farms.—*Chorus.*

To all these sad crimes there must be an ending,
   Secrets like these for ever can't last.
Say as you like, there is no defending
   The 'orrible tales we have heard in the past.—*Chorus.*

What did she think as she stood on the gallows,
  Poor little victims in front of her eyes?
Her heart if she 'ad one must have been callous,
  The rope round her neck—how quickly time flies!
    Chorus.

Down through the trap-door quickly disappearing,
  The old baby farmer to eternity 'ome.
The sound of her own death bell she was 'earing.
  Maybe she was sent to the cruel baby farm.
    Chorus.

I'M SEVENTEEN COME SUNDAY

Fairly fast.

(Solo.)
As I walk'd out one May morn-ing, One
Key Eb {:d |d :m |s :m |f :l |s :s
May morning so ear - - ly, I ov-er-took a
{|d :m |s :s |d' :-|s :s |d' :d' |d' :s

(Chorus)
hand-some maid, Just as the sun was ris-ing, With my
f :l |s :m |f :l |s :m |r :-|d :d .r

rum dum da, fal de rid-dle a, Oh—
m :s |m :-|s .f :m .r |d :d .m

right fall lal did-dle - i - do.
s :s |s :m .d |r :-|d :||

"Where are you going, my sweet pretty maid,
Where are you going, my honey?"
She answered me right cheerfully,
"With an errand for my mammy."
  With my rum dum da, etc.

221

" Will you take a man, my sweet pretty maid,
Will you take a man, my honey ? "
She answered me right cheerfully,
" I dare not, for my mammy."
   With my rum dum da, etc.

" How old are you, my sweet pretty maid,
How old are you, my honey ? "
She answered me right cheerfully,
" I'm seventeen come Sunday."
   With my rum dum da, etc.

" Will you come to my mammy's house,
When the moon shines bright and clearly,
And I'll come down and let you in,
And my mammy shall not hear me."
   With my rum dum da, etc.

AT THE HALT, ON THE LEFT

Quick march time.

222

WIDDICOMBE FAIR

With point.

(Solo.)
Tom Pearce, Tom Pearce, lend me your grey mare,

Key G
{ : s | d:—:d | m:—:r | t,:—.l, :s, | d:—}

(Chorus.)   (Solo.)
(All along,   down along,   out along lee,)   For I

{ d:—.d :d | m:—.r :d | t,:—.t,:d | r :— :s, }

want for to go— to Wid - de - combe Fair, Wi' Bill

{ d:—:d | m:r :d | t,:—.l, :s, | l,:—:s, .s, }

Brewer, Jan Stewer, Peter Gurney, Peter Davy, Dan'l

{ l,: — :s, | l,:—:s, | l,: — :s, | l,:—:s, }

(Chorus.)
Whiddon, Harry Hawk, Old Uncle Tom Cobleigh and

{ l,: — :s, | l,:—:s, | s,:f :m :r :—.d :t, }

all — Old Uncle Tom Cobleigh and all.

| s:—:—:—:f | m:—:f :m :r:—.d :t, | d:—:—:—:—:—||

And when shall I see again my grey mare?
By Friday soon or Saturday noon, etc.
   Wi' Bill Brewer, etc.

Then Friday came and Saturday noon,
Tom Pearce's old mare hath not trotted home.
   Wi' Bill Brewer, etc.

So Tom Pearce he got up to the top of the hill,
And he see'd his old mare a-making her will—
   Wi' Bill Brewer, etc.

223

So Tom Pearce's old mare her took sick and died,
And Tom he sat down on a stone and he cried—
  Wi' Bill Brewer, etc.

But this isn't the end of this shocking affair,
Nor, tho' they be dead, of the horrid career,
  Of Bill Brewer, etc.

When the wind whistles cold on the moor of a night,
Tom Pearce's old mare doth appear ghashly white—
  Wi' Bill Brewer, etc.

And all the night long be heard skirling and groans
From Tom Pearce's old mare in her rattling bones—
  Wi' Bill Brewer, etc.

THE BELLS OF HELL

Sincerely.

Key F
The bells of Hell go ting-a-ling-a-ling for
you and not for me. For
me the Angels sing-a-ling-a-ling, They've
got the goods for me O death where is thy sting-a-ling-a-ling? O
grave thy vic-to-ry? The bells of Hell go ting-a-ling-a-ling For
you and not for me.

THE RIO GRANDE

With spirit. At moderate speed.

(Solo.)

O, say were you ever in Ri-o-Grande,

Key E♭ {:s, | d :d | :d lm:m :m | r:d:r |d :-:- }

{| O'- you, Rio! - - It's there that the river runs
{|s :-:-:m |l:s :-:-:s | l :d' :l |s:f :m }

{| down golden sand, And we're bound for the Rio
{ f :s :f |m :d :r | m:- .f :m |r:s:- }

(Chorus.)

{| Grande. Then a-way love, a-way, 'Way-down
{ d :- :- |d:-:r | m:-:-:r :r |d:-:-:-:s :-:-:-:m }

{| Rio-- O, fare you well, my bonny young girl, For we're
{|l:s :-:-:s |l:d' :l |s:f :m |f :s :f |m :d :r }

{| bound for the Rio Grande.
{ m:- .f :m |r:s:- | d :-:-:-:-:|| }

Now you Bowery ladies, we'd have you to know,
   O, you Rio!
We're bound to the Southward, O Lord, let us go!
    For we're bound for the Rio Grande.
      Then away love, etc.

So it's pack up your donkey and get under way,
The girls we are leaving can take our half-pay.
    For we're bound, etc.

And good-bye, fare you well, all you ladies of town,
We've left you enough for to buy a silk gown.
    For we're bound, etc.

I

ALL THROUGH THE NIGHT

Slowly and religiously.

Key F
1. Deep the silence round us spreading,
All through the night; Dark the path that
we are treading All through the night.
Still the coming day discerning, By the hope within us burning, To the dawn our footsteps turning,
All through the night.

Star of Faith the dark adorning
    All through the night,
Leads us fearless toward the morning
    All through the night.
Though our hearts be wrapt in sorrow
From the hope of dawn we borrow
Promise of a glad to-morrow
    All through the night.

226

O GOOD ALE, THOU ART MY DARLING

With hearty humour.

The Land-lord he looks very big With his

high cock'd hat and his powder'd wig; Me-

thinks he looks both fair and fat, But

he may thank you and me for that, For 'tis

O, good ale, thou art my darling, And my joy both

night and morning.

The brewer brew'd thee in his pan,
The tapster draws thee in his can;
Now I with thee will play my part,
And lodge thee next unto my heart.
    For 'tis O, etc.

Thou oft hast made my friends my foes,
And often made me pawn my clothes;
But since thou art so nigh my nose,
Come up, my friend—and down he goes.
    For 'tis O, etc.

CHICKA-HANKA

At a moderate pace.

OWD JOE BRADDLES

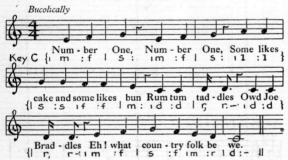

Number Two, Number Two
They all likes me and some likes you.
    Rum tum taddles, etc.

Number Three, Number Three
Some likes you but they all like me.
    Rum tum taddles, etc.

Number Four, Number Four
Some likes a gate but I like a door.
    Rum tum taddles, etc.

229

Number Five, Number Five
Some likes 'em dead but I likes 'em live.
    Rum tum taddles, etc.

Number Six, Number Six
Some likes posts but I likes sticks.
    Rum tum taddles, etc.

Number Seven, Number Seven
Is just the same as Number Eleven.
    Rum tum taddles, etc.

Number Eight, Number Eight
I like a door but some likes a gate.
    Rum tum taddles, etc.

Number Nine, Number Nine
Some likes ale but I likes wine.
    Rum tum taddles, etc.

Number Ten, Number Ten
Some likes a cock but I likes a 'en.
    Rum tum taddles, etc.

Number Eleven, Number Eleven
Is just the same as Number Seven.
    Rum tum taddles, etc.

SIR EGLAMORE

Quickly and with humour.

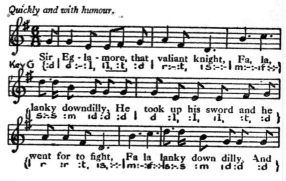

Key G

Sir Eg-la-more, that valiant knight, Fa, la, lanky downdilly, He took up his sword and he went for to fight, Fa la lanky down dilly, And

as he rode o'er, hill and dale, All armed with a
{m:f |s:–:m | l:–:s |f:–:m | r:–:d |t:–:l.}

coat of mail, Fa - lanky down, La - lanky down,
{ s:.s, |s:.:s:–:d:.r :m | f:–:–r:–.m :f }

Fa - la - lanky down dilly.
{|s:–:d |d:–.r :t, | d:–:d :–:– ||}

There starts a huge dragon out of his den, fa, la, etc.
Which had killed I know not how many men, fa, la, etc.
But when he see Sir Eglamore,
If you'd but heard how that dragon did roar, fa, la, etc.

This dragon had a plaguey hard hide,
Which could the strongest steel abide ;
But as the dragon yawning did fall,
He thrust his sword down hilt and all.

The dragon laid him down and roared,
The knight was sorry for his sword ;
The sword it was a right good blade,
As ever Turk or Spaniard made.

When all was done to the ale-house he went,
And presently his tuppence was spent ;
He was so hot with fighting the dragon,
And nought could quench his thirst but a flagon.

Well now let us pray for the King and the Queen,
And eke in London that may be seen,
As many knights and as many more,
And all as good as Sir Eglamore.

231

With fervour.

On this day, Earth shall ring With the song
children sing To the Son, Christ our King,
Born on earth to save us; Him the Father gave us.
I - de - o - o - o, I - de - o - o - o,
I - de - o glo - ri - a in ex - cel-sis De - o!

His the doom, ours the mirth,
When He came down to earth
Bethlehem saw His birth;
Ox and ass beside Him
From the cold would hide Him.—*I-de-o*, etc.

God's bright star, o'er His head,
Wise men three to Him led
Kneel they low by His bed,
Lay their gifts before Him,
Praise Him and adore Him.—*I-de-o*, etc.

On this day angels sing;
With their song earth shall ring
Praising Christ, Heaven's King,
Born on earth to save us;
Peace and love He gave us.—*I-de-o*, etc.

ALLELUIA, I'M A BUM

Very noisily.

1. A la-dy came out when I knocked at the door: "You'll get no-thing here, for I've seen you be-fore," Al-le-lu-ia, I'm a bum, bum, Al-le-lu-ia, bum a-gain, Al-le-lu-ia give us a hand-out to re-vive us a-gain.

"Oh why don't you work as the other fellows do?"
"How the hell can I work when there's no work to do?"
    Alleluia, etc.

"Oh why don't you pray for your daily bread?"
"If that's all I did I would damn soon be dead."
    Alleluia, etc.

"Oh I love my boss, he's a good friend of mine,
And that's why I am starving out on the bread line."
    Alleluia, etc.

N.B.—A "bum" is a migratory worker who picks up a living by wearing out his knuckles hammering at farmstead doors beseeching the flinty-hearted farmers to supply him with the necessaries of life in the form of a "hand-out."

CAN'T YOU DANCE THE POLKA?

Lively.

As I walk'd down the Broadway, one
Key C :s |d :m |s :d |f :l |, :d |

ev'ning in Ju-ly I met a maid who
|t :s |f :s |m :-:-:s |d' :d' |d' :s

axed my trade, "A sailor John," says
|t :l |l |:m |s :s |f :r

[Chorus].

I, And a-way you Santee, my dear Annie.
|d :r |m :f |s :-:-:d |f :l |, :s :-:f :- |m.m :-:l

O you New York girls, can't you dance the Polka?
|d :-l-:s |t |, :l |l :-s :-.s |f :- .t, |r :d |, :||

To Tiffany's I took her,
I did not mind expense;
I bought her two gold earrings,
They cost me fifty cents.
    And away, etc.

Says she, " You lime-juice sailor,
Now see me home my way."
But when we reached her cottage door
She unto me did say—
    And away, etc.

" My flash man—he's a Yankee,
With his hair cut short behind;
He wears a tarry jumper
And he sails on the Black-Ball line."
    And away, etc.

SÆTERJENTENS SÖNDAG

Slowly and sadly.　　　　　　　　　　　　　　　(*Ole Bull*)

Fain, fain would I my griefs impart,
　　Yet dare na for your anger;
But secret love will break my heart,
　　If I conceal it langer.
If thou refuse to pity me,
　　If thou shalt love anither,
When yon green leaves fa' frae the tree,
　　Around my grave they'll wither.

Robert Burns.

QUELLE EST CETTE ODEUR AGREABLE

Fairly quickly.

A Bethléem, dans une crêche
Il vient de vous naitre un sauveur;
Allons, que rien ne vous empêche
  D'adorer votre Redempteur.
A Bethléem, dans une crêche
Il vient de vous naitre un sauveur.

(*Note.*—If the smaller alternative notes are sung, this becomes the melody to which the following words are sung in "The Beggar's Opera.")

Fill every glass, for wine inspires us
And fires us with courage, love and joy!
Women and wine should life employ;
Is there ought else on earth desirous?
Fill every glass, for wine inspires us
And fires us with courage, love and joy!

" FIE, NAY, PRITHEE JOHN "

Fairly fast.

Round for three voices.
(Purcell.)

"Fie, nay, prithee John, Do not quarrel, man,

Key A♭ {|d :- .m |r .t, :s, | l, :- .d |t, .s, :m, }

Let's be merry and drink a - - bout."

{|f, :- .l |s, .m, :d | f, :s, | d, :— }

"You're a rogue, you cheated me, I'll

{|d .s :s |d |t, .s :s .t, }

prove before this company, I

{|l, .f :f |l, |s .m :m .s, }

caren't a farthing, Sir, for all you are so stout."

{|f, .r :r .f, |m .d :d .m, |r, :t, |d :— }

"Sir, you lie; I scorn your word or

{|s .m :d .l |f .r :t, .s }

any man that wears a sword, For

{|m .d :l, |f |r .t, :s, .m }

all your huff, who cares a damn, and

{|d .l :f, |r |t, .s, :m, .m }

who cares for you?"

{|l, :s, .f |m, :— || }

237

HEY, HO, TO THE GREENWOOD

WILLIAM BYRD

With elation, and fairly quickly. (Canon for three voices.)

238

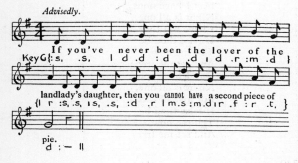

FRAGMENT

239

MARISHKA

Rather slowly and passionately.

1. Ma - rish - ka, Ma - rish - ka, Look not at me, Ma - ry. Thy glan - ces are lan - ces, With their darts be wa - ry. *All my joy they've chas'd a - way, And my peace has flown; My heart pines with one de - sire, To be thine own. *Repeat from double bar.*

The sunlight, the moonlight,
I know not in thy sight;
The day and the dark night
Lie within thine eyes bright.
Day I have none,
Night is all one,
I have but thee;
If false thou be
Tell me now,
And set me free;
Day I have none,
Night is all one,
For love of thee;
If false thou be,
Tell me now,
And set me free.

240

THE OLD MAN THAT LIVED NEAR HELL

Loud and lively.

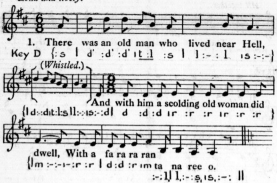

1. There was an old man who lived near Hell,

Key D {:s | d' :d' :d' |t :l | s | l :–: l |s :–:–}

(Whistled.)

And with him a scolding old woman did

{|d :d :t :l :s |l :–:s :–:d | d | d :d :d |r :r | :r |r :r | :r }

dwell, With a fa ra ra ran

{|m :–:–:r :r | d :d :r |m ta na ree o.

:–:l|l :–:s |s :–: ||

The *devil* came to him one *day* at the plough,
" Its *one* of your family I do want now."

" It *isn't* your son that *I* do crave,
But it *is* your oul' wife, its her I maun ha'e."

" *Tak'* her awa' wi *all* ma guid hert,
Hoping that you and her never will part."

He *hoisted* her up on the *oul'* de'ils back,
And like a bold pedlar he carried his pack.

Its *when* they came unto Hell's door,
He then threw her down with a clash on the floor.

There were *seven* de'ils there tied *up* wi' chains,
She lifted her crutch and she knocked out their brains.

There were *three* de'ils more holdin' *up* the wall,
" *Tak'* her awa' she will kill us all.

" She's *not* fit for heaven an' *nay*ther for Hell,
We must *build* her house, she maun live by her sel'."

" And *on* her dresser, she maun *have* some delf ;
If you *want* any more, you maun sing it yourself ! "

241

THE THREE CROWS

All together.

There were three crows sat on a tree, O
Key Gmi {: ₁l, l m, ,l : l, ,₁t, ₁ d ,t : d ,₁l, }

Billy Ma - gee Magar - - There
{l s,, s,, s, :s, ,,m, ₁s, :— ,₁l, }

were three crows sat on a tree, O
{l m, ₃ l, : l, ,,t, d ,t, :d ,,r }

Billy Ma - gee Magar - - There
{lm ,m ,m :m ,,d ₁m :— ,,d }

were three crows sat on a tree, And
{l m ,,m :m ,,d ₁r ,,r :r ,,t, }

they were black as black could be, And they
{l d ,,d :d ,,l, ₁t, ,,t, :t, ,d ,,r }

all flapped their wings and cried, *Caw, Caw, Caw,—*
{lm :r ₃ ,,r ₁d ,,d :t, ₁ *(Imitate Crows),* }

Billy Magee Magar, And they
{l l, ,,l, ,,l, :l, ,,l, ₁l, :d ,,r }

all flapped their wings and cried,
{lm ₃ :r ,,r ₁d ,,d :t, }

Billy Magee Magar - -
{l l, ,,l, ,,l, :l, ,,l ₁l, :— ‖ }

242

Said one old crow unto his mate,
" What shall we do for our grub to ate ? "

" There lies a horse on yonder plain,
Whose by some cruel butcher slain."

" We'll perch ourselves on his backbone,
And pick his eyes out one by one."

" The meat we'll eat before it's stale,
Till nought remain but bones and tail."

FRANKIE AND JOHNNIE

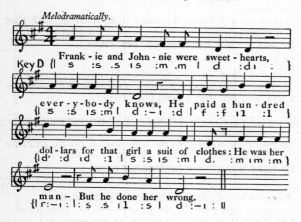

Frankie went to the beer-shop, she ordered a bottle of beer,
She said, " Now, Mr. Bar-tender-man, have you seen my
Johnnie here?
He was my man—but he done me wrong!"

The Bar-tender said, " Frankie, I can't tell you no lie ;
Your Johnnie was here an hour ago, with a girl called Alice
Fly :
She's pinched your man—who done you wrong ! "

Frankie went to the pawn-shop—she didn't go there for
fun—
When she came out of that pawn-shop, she had a great, big,
wonderful gun
To shoot that man—who done her wrong !

Frankie went to the Dance-hall, she rang the Dance-hall
bell,
She said, " Clear out, you people, I'm going to blow this
man to hell
For he was my man—and he done me wrong ! "

Frankie shot Johnnie the first time ; Frankie shot Johnnie
twice ;
Frankie shot Johnnie the third time, and she took that
gambler's life.
He was her man—but he done her wrong !

" Oh ! Roll me over easy, roll me over slow,
That bullet in my poor left side it sure does hurt me so—
I was her man—but I done her wrong ! "

Bring out your hundred-dollar coffin, bring out your rubber
tyred hack
To take poor Johnnie to the cemetery, never for to bring
him back.
He was her man—but he done her wrong !

Now, the moral of this story is very plain to all—
Be careful you young ladies or you sure will have a fall :
Just watch these men—or they'll do you wrong ! ! !

MISS BAILEY

Fast but sad.
(Solo.)

A captain bold in Hali - fax that dwelt in country quar - ters, De - ceived a maid who hanged herself one morning in her gar - ters, His wicked conscience smited him, he lost his stomach dai-ly, He took to drinking turpentine, and thought upon Miss

(Chorus.)

Bai - ley, O, Miss Bailey, un - fortunate Miss Bai-ley, O Miss Bailey, un - fortunate Miss Bailey.

245

SPANISH LADIES

Raucously.
(Solo.)

Fare - well and a - - dieu to you, Fair Spanish

Key G {: s, | d .d :r | d .-r :m | f :r :d

La - dies, Fare - well and a - dieu to you,

{| t .l, :s, | s, | r :r :m | r :- :r .m }

Ladies of Spain, For we've re - ceived or - ders to

{| f :m :r | s: :m .f | s: s: :s | m .r :d :r .m}

sail for old Eng - land, But we hope in a

{| f :r :d | t .l, :s, | :s .f | m :m :m}

(Chorus.)

short time to see you a - - gain. We'll rant and we'll

{| f :r :d | t :l, :t, | d :- :s, | d :d :r }

roar, all o'er the wild o - - cean, We'll rant and we'll

{| d :- :r .m | f :r :d | t .l, :s, :s, | r :r :m }

roar, all o'er the wild seas, Un -

{| r :- :r .m | f :m :r | s :- : m .f }

til we strike sound - ings in the Channel of Old

{| s :s :s | m .r :d :r .m | f .f :r :d }

Eng - land, From Ushant to Scil - ly is thir ty five

{| t .l, :s, :s .f | m :m :m | f :r :d | t :l, :t, }

leagues.

{| d :- :- ||

246

We hove our ship too, with the wind at sou'west, boys,
  We hove our ship for to strike soundings clear;
Then filled the main topsail and bore right away, boys,
  And straight up the Channel our course we did steer.
            We'll rant and we'll roar, etc.

The first land we made was a point called the Dodman,
  Next Rame Head off Plymouth, Start, Portland and
    Wight,
We sailed then by Beachy, by Fairlee and Dung'ness,
  Then bore straight away for the South Foreland Light.

The signal was made for the Grand Fleet to anchor,
  We clewed up our topsails, stuck out tacks and sheets,
We stood by our stoppers, we brailed in our spanker,
  And anchored ahead of the noblest of fleets.

Then let every man here toss off a full bumper,
  Then let every man here toss off his full bowl,
For we will be jolly and drown melancholy,
  With a health to each jovial and true-hearted soul.

THE JONES BOYS

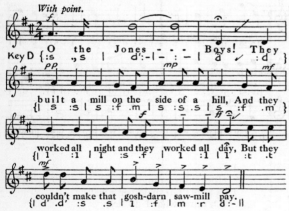

247

A-ROVING

Rollicking.
(Solo.)

Key F

In Plymouth Town there lived a maid,

(Chorus.)   (Solo.)

(Bless you young wo-men) In Plymouth Town there

(Chorus.)   (Solo.)

lived a maid, (O, mind what I - 3 - do say) In

Plymouth Town there lived a maid, and

she was mis-tress of her trade, I'll go no more a-

(Chorus.)

ro - - ving with you fair maid. A - ro - - ving, a-

ro - - ving, Since rov-ing's been my ru-i-in, I'll

go no more a- ro - - ving with you fair, maid.

I took this fair maid for a walk
(Bless you young women)
I took this fair maid for a walk
(O, mind what I do say)

I took this fair maid for a walk
  And we had such a loving talk,
I'll go no more a-roving with you fair maid,

Chorus.
And didn't I tell her stories too, etc.
Of the gold we found in Timbuctoo, etc.

But when we'd spent my blooming screw, etc.
She cut her stick and vanished too, etc.

LILLIBURLERO

In rousing march time.

(Solo.)   (Chorus.)

Dat we shall have a new de-pu-tie, Lilli-bur-ler-o.
Key D {|d :r :d |m:-:m| r :m :r ı f:-.| m :s :d ı f:- :m}

(Solo.)

bullen a la. Ho! brother Teague dost hear de decree.
{|r :d.t,ıd:-|d :r :d ı m:- :m| r :m ı r ı f:-.|}

(Chorus.)   (Chorus.)

Lilli-bur-ler-o bullen a la. Le-ro, le-ro,
{|m :s :d ı f:-:m| r :d :t,ıd:-|d':- :t ı d:-:s }

lilli-bur-le-ro, lilli-bur-le-ro bullen a la--
{|s :l ı t.a ıl:-:s | s :l :t ı d':s ı l | s :f :m ı r:-:s}

le-ro, le-ro, le-ro, -le-ro lilli-bur-le-ro
{|l :s :f ı m:f :s | l:s :t ı m:f :s | l :d' :d ı f:- :m}

bullen a la.
{| r :d :t ı d:-:-||

HERE IS JOY FOR EV'RY AGE

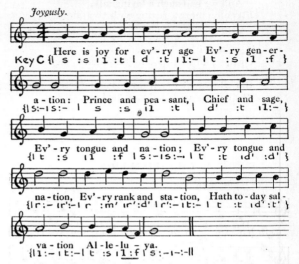

Joyously.

Here is joy for ev'ry age Ev'ry gen-er-
Key C {| s :s | 1 :t | d :t | 1:– | t :s | 1 :f }

a-tion: Prince and pea-sant, Chief and sage,
{| s:– | s:– | s :s | 1 :t | d' :t | 1:– }

Ev'-ry tongue and na-tion; Ev'-ry tongue and
{| t :s | 1 :f | s:– | s:– | t :t | d' :d' }

na-tion, Ev'-ry rank and sta-tion, Hath to-day sal-
{| r:– | r:– | r :m' | r':d' | r':– | t:– | t :t | d':t' }

va-tion Al-le-lu-ya.
{| 1:– | t:– | t :s | 1:f | s:–:–:–:|| }

When the world drew near its close
  Came our Lord and Leader:
From the lily sprang the rose,
  From the bush the cedar;
From the bush the cedar,
From the judg'd the pleader,
From the faint the feeder;
  Alleluya.

God, that came on earth this morn,
  In a manger lying,
Hallow'd birth by being born,
  Vanquish'd death by dying;
Vanquish'd death by dying,
Rallied back the flying,
Ended sin and sighing;
  Alleluya.

AYE WAUKIN' O!

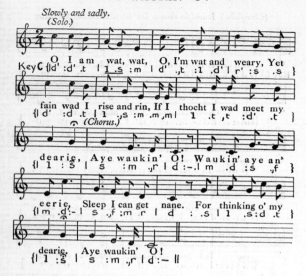

Spring's a pleasant time,
Flowers of ev'ry colour,
The water rins o'er the heugh,
And I long for my lover.
       Aye waukin' O! etc.

When I sleep I dream,
When I wauk I'm eerie;
Sleep I can get nane
For thinking on my dearie,

Lanely night comes on,
A' the lave are sleepin',
I think on my true love,
And I bleer my een wi' greetin'.

Robert Burns.

251

(Cheerfully.) *Round for three or four mixed voices and two basses.*

Key E♭

Sum - er is i - cu - men in——— Lhu - de sing cuc -

cu   Grow - eth sed, And   blow - eth med, And

spring - 'th the wd - e nu. Sing cuc - - cu.

Aw - e blet - eth af - ter lomb, Lhouth af - ter cal - ve

cu,   Bul - luc ster - teth, Buck - e vert - eth,

Mu - rie sing cu - cu,   cu - cu,— cuc—cu, Wel

sing - es thu cuc - cu. Ne — swik thu na - ver

Back to the beginning.

nu;

252

These four bars are repeated ad infinitum by two male voices.

cuc-cu,   cuc-cu   cuc-cu   cuc-cu—

* The 2nd, 3rd and 4th voices enter in turn, when the previous part has reached the beginning of the third bar.

I WISH I WERE

As if you really were.

Key F

I wish I were a-- El - e - phan-

ti - a - phus - And could pick off the co - co - nuts with my

nose-- But oh! I am not - (a - las I

can - not be--) an El - e - phan - ti - El - e - phan -

ti - a - phus - But I'm a cock - roach - And I'm a

wa - ter - bug - I can crawl a - round and hide be - hind the

sink.

I wish I were a
Rhinosceréeacus
And could wear an ivory toothpick in my nose.
But, oh ! I am not,
(Alas ! I cannot be)
A Rhinoscóri-
Rhinosceréeacus.
But I'm a beetle
And I'm a pumpkin-bug,
I can buzz and bang my head against the wall.

I wish I were a
Hippopópotamus
And could swim the Tigris and the broad Gangés.
But, oh ! I am not,
(Alas ! I cannot be)
A hippopópo-
Hippopopótamus.
But I'm a grasshopper
And I'm a katydid,
I can play the fiddle with my left hind-leg.

I wish I were a
Levileviathan
And had seven hundred knuckles in my spine.
But, oh ! I am not,
(Alas ! I cannot be)
A Levi-ikey-
A Levi-ikey-mo.
But I'm a firefly
And I'm a lightning-bug,
I can light cheroots and gaspers with my tail.

(*And so ad infinitum.*)

" Play ! "
Any Umpire.

∽∽∽∽∽∽∽∽∽∽∽∽∽∽∽∽∽∽∽∽

PLAY!

∽∽∽∽∽∽∽∽∽∽∽∽∽∽∽∽∽∽∽∽

Y O U *and* I *and* O U R F R I E N D S *are gathered together after supper in the House where we happen to be spending the Week-end. Our Names are* A L I C E, L A U R A, F E R D I N A N D, C Y N T H I A, R O B E R T, L U C I A N, D O R C A S, J E R E M Y, G E O R G E, H A M B L E T O N, *and* J O H N. H A M B L E T O N *is a Man. Most of us are smoking,* L A U R A *is wistfully but vainly shuffling a pack of cards,* G E O R G E *is scribbling furiously, and* J O H N *is committing an occasional sentence to paper.* O N E O F U S *is still sulking over that disputed Point in Rounders which upset us all just after Tea.*

C Y N T H I A (*Who hates Tensions*): Let's play something.

J E R E M Y: Yes, do let's.

L U C I A N: It's all jolly well to say Let's. We'll never agree what.

H A M B L E T O N: What a wet blanket you are, Lucian! I'm ready for Simply Anything! Somebody suggest something.

L A U R A: There's a rather nice game called

SUGGESTIONS

We just sit as we are, and I say something I'm thinking of, like " Cards," and Ferdinand says whatever it suggests to him, like " Patience," and Cynthia says what *that* suggests to *her*, like " Monument," and then Robert might suggest " R.I.P." or " Nelson," and Lucian might say " Winkle " —or " Keys "——

L U C I A N: I wouldn't.

L A U R A: Well, we go on like that till we've done enough, and then we begin to unwind the chain of suggestions backwards, saying in turns What was suggested by What, and anyone who makes a slip or gets stuck, loses a life ; and anyone who loses two, or three lives, as agreed on, is dead. And at the end you see who's left alive.

K   257

HAMBLETON: How Perfectly Splendid! But if we're *only* going to sit and talk, let's try a

FREE ASSOCIATION TEAM-RACE

It's based on Psycho-Analysis, you know, which is always jolly. Two Captains pick up sides, which line up face to face, and there's a Timekeeper-Scorer-Referee who says Go! Then the Captain of the side in talks as fast as he can about anything or nothing, while the Referee counts the words : he can talk sentences, or any jumble of disconnected words he pleases (that's where the Free Association comes in, *and* the Psycho-Analysis, because you're always revealing your Inner Life by saying things like " postprandial flower-pot puff ! " you know), but he mustn't take one word and stick to it, like " me-me-me-me-me ! " As soon as his flow stops (and it *will*, because of some Inhibition, you know), the next in his team takes it up until *he* sticks ; and so on, down the line, and round again if necessary, until the Referee calls Time !—which is anything previously arranged, from two to five minutes. Then the other side goes in ; you can have any number of innings you like ; and whichever side says most words wins.

FERDINAND: And at the end all our Complexes have been given away. A dangerous game, my dear Ham. I prefer

THE ANIMAL AND STICK GAME

Two sides, face to face, like yours, but no Referee. Each Captain has a stick. A member of one side calls the name of any animal, bird, fish, or insect, beginning with A, and his Captain instantly begins to count 10 aloud (not *too* fast), thumping the floor with his stick at each count. Before he reaches 10, some member of the opposing side must retaliate with another creature beginning with A, on which the second Captain begins to count and thump, while the first side thinks of a new beast. Captains are allowed to call like the rest ; but if two members of a side call out different names together, the opposing side may instantly bag the second name given. When one team wins, because the other has run out of

A's, it may choose a member of the losing team and add
him to their number. The second bout begins with B,
and the game continues through the alphabet, until all of
one side has been absorbed by the other. No penalty is
incurred for Fake Names of animals, and if, when stumped
for an N, you *can* bring off " Nicaragua " unchallenged,
you may; but on the whole these should not be indulged
in too often, and, once disproved, the Opposing Captain
takes up the count where the bluff interrupted it.

DORCAS: Might not this game also be played with
the names of Flowers, or Towns, or Famous People, as
well as Animals ?

FERDINAND (*kindly*) : Yes, Dorcas, it might.

DORCAS: All these can be played as Paper-Games, too
—I like nice quiet Paper-Games. When you play

FAMOUS PEOPLE ON PAPER

you have two or three minutes for writing as many Famous
People, or Flowers, or Things in the Room, or whatever
you like, beginning with a certain letter, and you read
them out in turn and score marks; if ten people are
playing, nobody scores for a name everybody has thought
of, but if 9 people have it you each score 1, and if 8 people,
they each score 2, and so on. Or else there's

CONSEQUENCES

HAMBLETON: So there is, by Jove! But if we
must play a Paper Game,

BOOK REVIEWS

is better. It's played like Consequences, but first you
invent the Title of a Book—say " Crimson Nights "—
turn down, and pass on; on the paper you receive you
write a sub-title, say, " Or 366 Ways of Cooking Lentils ";
round three is the Author's name, real or imaginary;
round four a brief extract from the book, poetry or prose;
round five another extract (for contrast); six, extract from
a review of the book; seven, name of Journal the review
comes from; eight, extract from another review (contrast
again !); nine, and last, name of Journal.

259

FERDINAND: Not bad for a round or two. No Paper Game should be allowed to pall. It's their chief danger.

REDUCED ANECDOTES

makes a variation. Each player writes some anecdote, or incident, in 80 words, and passes it on; he cuts down the anecdote he receives to 40 words, writing it out below the first one, leaving any sort of sense he can make without changing the order of the words or introducing any new ones; after the pass, this is reduced to 20, then to 10, finally to 5. The anecdotes are passed once more, and the result read aloud, from top to bottom; or vice versa. Papers should be folded so that the players only see the lines they are to reduce.

LAURA: Poetry is so much nicer than Prose, don't you think? Why not play

BOUTS-RIMÉS?

Give the rhyme-endings of a poem, and let everyone fit a verse to them in a given time; or else

COMBINATION VERSES

fixing a meter and rhyme-scheme, and passing the papers like in Consequences, with the last line but one hidden; or

LIMERICKS

on given places or people; or

"CLERIHEWS"

on your personal friends, with nice slack metres and sly points like
> " Sir Christopher Wren
> Was going to dine with some men.
> He said, ' If anybody calls,
> Say I'm designing Saint Paul's ' "

—you remember?

HAMBLETON (*hurriedly, while she pauses for breath*): For a Personal Game you can't beat

PLAY!

PERSONAL ANALOGIES

You write the names of those present perpendicularly down your paper, and each in turn chooses a subject—a Colour, Food, Drink, Street, Material, etc.—which are written horizontally across the top. Then everybody sets to and writes against each person's name the nearest analogy he can think of in the different subjects. They're read out afterwards, and no one need explain *why* he thinks you are Scarlet or Putty-Coloured, or like Suet-Pudding or Pêche Melba, or Bond Street or the City Road. It's a good way of paying compliments and old scores, you see——

DORCAS: I shouldn't like it at all. I can't think of things out of my own head. But I know a brand new game that's much easier, called

QUALITIES

You make a list of qualities, good, bad and indifferent. There's one at the end of the " Week-End Book " (*picks it up and exhibits page* 350). You see, these pages are ruled out ready to play on. You draw lots, decide who shall be the subject and he has to give himself marks for each quality and then pass the book on to the rest of us in turn to mark him. Supposing it were Hambleton, he would write in the left-hand column *Hambleton* on *Hambleton* and put his own markings on the same line under each quality ; then there would be *Cynthia* on *Hambleton* on the next line, and so on. And when we had all finished with him, he would have to read out the verdicts and if you like even work out his average for each quality. Or else we could play it two by two, each marking himself and the other player.

LUCIAN: That's a *chic* " confessions book," but it's not a game.

CYNTHIA (*firmly removing the " Week-End Book "*) : Anyhow I propose to keep my copy for collecting people's opinions of me.

LUCIAN: " To see ourselves as others see us ? " I wouldn't have it at a " giftie " !

HAMBLETON (*with point*) : When *I* mark you——

FERDINAND: Pax !

JEREMY (*diffidently producing a second copy*) : Dorcas——
DORCAS: Oh, do let's !
JEREMY : It'll be quieter in the dining-room. (*Exeunt.*)
LUCIAN (*whistles a few bars of Mendelssohn's most well-known march*).
FERDINAND (*confiscates Hambleton's pencil and Cynthia's book*) : If you *must* play dangerous games, do it on Sunday evening ; we don't want to disintegrate just yet. What about trying a revised version of Famous People called

WHO AM I ?

The Scorer first writes the names of lots of *very* Famous People, and Characters in Books, and Notorious Recent Criminals, and all that, on separate bits of paper, and has lots of pins, and a scoring-sheet with all the names of the other players. They line up before him, and he pins a name on each one's back and says Go ! Your object is to find out who you are. You may rush up to anybody, make him look at your back, and fire off three questions to which the only answers are " Yes " and " No " : Such as " Am I a Man ? " " Am I a Myth ? " " Am I a Foreigner ? " When your three questions are answered, you must answer three of his in return ; then you part, and grab somebody else, carrying on your investigation from the information gained. You mustn't ever ask more than three questions from a chap at one go. When you know who you are you tell the Scorer ; he replaces your old name with a new one, and scores a mark to you. The game stops when everybody's hoarse, or the Scorer runs out of names ; and the one who has guessed himself oftenest wins. If you get such a hard name that you're really stumped, you may ask the Scorer for a new one ; but you lose a mark for it.
CYNTHIA: It sounds like a Parrot-House. A much prettier way of playing people is

WHO ARE THEY ?

Two of us go outside and decide who we'll be, and return to hold a conversation in front of the others, always talking in character, but of course not mentioning our names.

PLAY!

When you're guessed, two others go out. It's the best opportunity I know for bringing nice people together who would have liked to meet, but can't: Hobbs and Medusa, you know, or Dempsey and Little Nell——

HAMBLETON: Topping! But if we've *got* to have a Conversation Game, there's always

SALTED ALMONDS

It's called that, because it takes place between two people who are supposed to meet at a dinner-table. Before they meet, A goes outside, and B is given three statements or remarks, invented by the audience, which he must engineer as naturally as possible into the dinner-table conversation: such as that he never *can* remember whether it's pronounced Bill Sykes or Bill Seeks; and that the best cure for aeroplane-sickness is equal parts of Fuller's Earth and Petroleum; and that the First Carpet-Slippers were worked by Lady Jane Grey for Roger Ascham. Then A comes in, the two sit side by side, and they begin to talk. A's job is to head off B's attempts to steer the conversation towards his statements, though A doesn't know what they are. The game ends when B makes his third statement.

ALICE: Isn't that a sort of acting, like

CHARADES?

Charades always make me so nervous.

CYNTHIA: Oh, I *love* Charades! But can you bear

DUMB CRAMBO

better, Dorcas? It can be just as nice as Charades if you dress up for it, and arrange dumb-show scenes to act, and bring in *heaps* of rhymes at once, so that the audience must guess your words while you're trying to guess theirs. I remember once, when the real word was " Speak " (which of course we couldn't), and before we'd guessed it we'd done Greek meeting Greek over a Game of Bezique, and a Beak giving a Freak a Week for a Tweak on the Cheek (of the Freak's Wife, you know), and a Teak on a Bleak Creek on the Mozambique——

HAMBLETON: I *wish* I'd been there! Still, if we're *going* to act in dumb show for the Audience to guess

263

PLAY!
HISTORY IN PANTOMIME

is the Thing ! There's no end to what you can do—Alfred
and the Cakes, and the Murder of the Little Princes, and
the Arrival in London of Mary Pickford, and the Cup-
Finals—only p'r'aps those last two are too much alike.
Canute's a good one, with two of us lying flat on the floor
in the passage under a sheet for the Sea, and surging in
through the door to Canute's feet.

C Y N T H I A : If we are going to do any play-acting why
not do something really worth while, such as

DRAMATIZED BALLADS

They make the most thrilling little plays and any one with
a dramatic sense can " produce " them. (*Glancing through
the " Week-End Book.*") Look at the " Earl of Moray "—
what a marvellous love-and-hate story one could do in
dumb show to lead up to the critical moment when it breaks
into words !

H A M B L E T O N : (*looking over her shoulder*) : But
there are so few speeches, most of it is in story form ; and
besides the scene changes too often.

C Y N T H I A (*getting warmed up to her ruling passion*) :
But you have to choose which scenes to act and describe
the rest, just as in dramatized novels. And as for the
story-teller, you can change a word or two here and there
and split up his part between the speaking characters or
invent fresh ones to fill in the story. A ballad is only a
text for a play. For instance, in " The Queens Marie "
you would have various gossips about the court, being
friendly or unfriendly, and telling the first part of the
story, say until Marie comes back from drowning her
baby ; and——

R O B E R T (*who is afraid of* C Y N T H I A ' S *energy*) : I
dare say ! But if we *must* be highbrow let's try to get some
improvement out of it. I'm for Pelman's Infallible Road
to Success or Train Your Powers of Observation.

M O S T O F U S : Help !

R O B E R T : Don't be frightened—I only mean

PLAY!

THE TRAY-GAME.

Someone fills a tray with twenty objects usual to any room
—a pencil, handkerchief, book, nib, and what not——

FERDINAND: How do you get the What-not on the
tray?

ROBERT (*kindly*): The tray is set down in the middle of
the other players, who stare at it for twenty or thirty seconds
only, when it is removed. The Tray-Filler (and Time-
Keeper) then calls Go! and the players have two minutes
in which to write down all they can remember. The longest
list wins. That's a Sight-and-Memory Test. Then you
might have

SENSE-TESTS

the blindfolded players being given different things to
taste and recognize—borax, cornflour, cocoa, quinine, and
what not——

LAURA: However do you——?

ROBERT (*kindly*): That's a Taste-Test. For Feeling,
you might be given velvet to touch, and wood, and dough,
and rose-leaves—not to be *handled*, merely caressed——

LUCIAN: Æsthete!

ROBERT: Or for Hearing, a series of sounds made by,
say, an egg-whisk, a metronome, a police-rattle, opening a
window, striking a match, and what—and so on. The
Tests must be pre-arranged by some fairly ingenious
person.

FERDINAND: Have you ever tried

LOOKING AT YOUR FEET THROUGH THE WRONG END OF THE OPERA-GLASSES

while you try to walk, step by step, one foot put straight in
front of the other, down a string laid on the floor?

LUCIAN: No.

FERDINAND: Oh.

ALICE: *I* like something active and exciting.

HIDE AND SEEK IN THE DARK

is a real Thrill!

HAMBLETON: Oh, gaudy! But

K*   265

SARDINES

is gaudier still. Only one player hides, all the others seek ; the first to find him hides with him, the next to find *them* squashes in alongside, and so on till everybody's hiding in the same spot but one Seeker. Come on, who'll hide first ?

FERDINAND : Let's stay by the fire, Ham ; if Alice must have action, there's

POTATO-AND-SPOON TEAM-RACES

six potatoes a side, laid out on the floor, basket each end into which potatoes are dropped as soon as picked up, no player to shove his potato against any foreign matter while endeavouring to pick it up ; as soon as he's done his six, he lays out the potatoes again rapidly, and passes his spoon to the next member of his team. Or else, there's

TISHY-TOSHY.

ALICE : Sounds silly.

FERDINAND : It's far better than it sounds. Indeed an early version of the game is said to have taught Bosanquet the googly. You need a table (rectangular, the largest possible) and a tennis-ball. Two players stand at opposite ends, and throw the ball to each other in turn ; the Server may roll, bounce, or full pitch the ball, but it must not drop off the sides of the table (only off the ends) and must only leave the table between imaginary parallel lines continuing the sides of the table. The Receiver may not put his hands over the table, or touch it with his hands or any part of his person. If he does so, or if he fails to catch the ball, the Server scores one point. If the Receiver catches the ball lawfully, neither scores. But the Receiver score as point if the Server sends the ball off the sides of the table. Game is for any number of points agreed upon—say five. The very expert (which we wont be) can make a rule to use one hand only, or to bar catches made against the body.

HAMBLETON : Capital ! But if it *is* to be a Table-Game, we all know

266

more or less, and can all play it at once. Only before we start, we ought to agree whether orders can only be legally obeyed when given by one of the Captains ; and if the team which is hiding the Sixpence obeys any other order, it ought to forfeit the Sixpence. The " In " team, which is hiding the coin, must put up its hands the instant the opposing Captain calls " Up-Jenkyns ! " but he ought to allow them at least five seconds before he calls. He can keep their hands in the air as long as he likes, for examination purposes ; the " Down " calls are " Down-Jenkyns " (hands can be put down as players please) ; " Smashums ! " (hands must be crashed down on the table) ; " Crawlers ! " (hands placed quietly on the table, and fingers quietly undone till the hands lie flat) ; " Open Windows " (hands must lie on the table with all the fingers, but not the thumbs, apart) ; and " Lobster-Pots " (finger-tips only to rest on the table, and fingers to be held at right-angles to the palm). In removing the hands, again, only the Captain's order must be obeyed ; but he should allow free and fair consultation to his own side first. Scores can be played for, by the number of separate " wins," or the show of hands on the table when the Sixpence is discovered. *Before* the game starts, all rings and spurs to be removed. *After* the game, let the provider of the sixpence see that he gets it back !

L A U R A : Up-Jenkyns always gives me sore thumbs. I must say I like nice quiet games like

GO.

T H E O T H E R S (*kindly*) : Go, Laura ?
L A U R A : Yes, really. It's Japanese. You play it with coffee and haricot beans, *ad lib.*, on a board, or piece of paper, ruled into squares, 29 by 31 ; the two players play one bean at a time, in turns, on any square they like ; you want to enclose your opponent's bean in a diagonal square of your own like this :

which entitles you to remove the enclosed bean. When one player has the whole board covered with his beans, he wins. There's only one rule, called Ko——
THE OTHERS: Ko, Laura?
LAURA: Yes, really. Didn't I tell you it was Japanese? Suppose you get a situation like *this* :

Haricot could play in the empty square A, and remove Coffee from B; but then, you see, Coffee could immediately play in B again, and remove Haricot from A; and so on, for ever. To prevent this, the Rule is that in this particular position the *first* encircler keeps his opponent's bean, and cannot have his own retaken in that grouping. It's a very good game. In Japan proletarians and women were forbidden to play it; because it wastes too much of a wage-slaye's time, and females are quite cunning enough already!
ALICE: That sounds unprincipled! But it reminds me of

GO-BANG.

You play *that* on the same sort of board, with coloured beans or counters in turns, and the object is to get five of your own colour in a row, in any direction, straight or diagonal. It's rather fascinating, and it *may* be Japanese too.

268

HAMBDETON: I *do* like the Japanese! Still, if we're *going* to play a game on a board

NINE MEN'S MORRIS

is pure English. The players have nine men apiece—beans, or anything to show a difference—and if you look at the end-papers of the " Week-End Book " you'll see the sort of board it's played on. It has 24 bases which, read horizontally and perpendicularly, form 16 lines of three bases each. Players begin by placing their men alternately on any base that is vacant, and the great object (it's a sort of glorified Noughts and Crosses) is to get three of your men in a line, either up or down. As soon as you succeed, you can "Pound " any one of your opponent's men, and remove it from the board. When the placing of the men on the board is completed (during which one or more men may have been Pounded) you go on by moving in turns from base to base ; a man can only move to a base adjacent to his own, and then only if it is unoccupied by another man. You can't take a man by moving on to his base, you can only take a man when you get a line of three. In this way, one of the players is presently reduced to three men, and when that happens he has the privilege of " hopping " from one base to another—that is, any of his men can " hop " to *any* base he likes, so long as it is vacant ; but it need not be next the base he has just left. The player with more than three men must still go on moving in the old way, until he also is reduced to three. The game ends, of course, when one player has only two men left, which nobody but Einstein could make a line of three of—see ?

ROBERT: I might—if Ferdinand hadn't bagged the " Week-End Book." What a lot of breath you've wasted, Ham. *You* haven't made a suggestion yet, George. Drop that Epic, and speak up.

GEORGE: Young friend, I will. This Epic is entirely in your interests. While *you* have been making disagreements as to what you'll play to-night, *I* have been drawing up agreements as to what we'll play to-morrow. I have here a Thesis on certain arbitrary rules for vexed questions

PLAY!

in Rounders, Small Hockey, Small Cricket, and Tierce, to avoid all future unp——
L U C I A N : Huh !
G E O R G E : Hum—discussion. As we all know the general rules of these games, I deal only with special points, and the spirit in which they are played. Allow me :

ROUNDERS.

" In this favourite game, if a batsman's hit is caught, he only, and not the whole side, is out, unless a contrary convention has been made. (If you want to speed up the game, make such a convention.) Otherwise, a side is out only if, for any reason, there is none of the batting side home to bat. Further, a member of the batting side is out if he is touched by a ball, thrown or in the hand, when not on the base.
" A player who is out may be redeemed by his side on payment of one rounder, if the side is in credit—otherwise as soon as a rounder is scored. This privilege cannot be postponed until it is proved that there is a tactical necessity for the redemption (i.e. the emergency of the lack of batsmen to keep the side going, all others being on bases).
" A player on a base may feint to go to another base and retire to his former ; but he must regain this before he is touched.
" The Bowler may feint and, instead of bowling, throw to a fielder ; but if the ball leaves his hand, it counts as one of the three throws out of which one must be a ' good ' ball to the Batsman.
" A ' good ' ball is a slow ball between shoulder and knee of Batsman, outside his body to the offside, and within one yard of his body. If the Bowler delivers three ' bad ' balls, the penalty is a Rounder to the other side. There should, if possible, be a Referee who would decide on good and bad balls, and all other points. If a batsman fails to hit any of three good balls, he is out.
" A hit behind the Batsman is not a ' good ' hit ; it counts as a Good Ball not taken.
" A Player on a base may run for a ' bad ' ball, or for a ' good ' ball not run for by the Batsman.

270

" All running between basesis stopped by the bowler bouncing the ball. The runner must go unmolested to his nearest base.

" Players on the batting side must *never* run inside the bases, whatever these may be—trees, walking-sticks, hats, or coats. In the latter cases, bases should not be stood upon.

" As anything may be used for bases, so it may for the tools of the game ; but a tennis-ball, and the handle of a walking-stick, are not only the best in themselves, but are generally available."

" SMALL " CRICKET

" I call this ' Small ' Cricket, as opposed to the Greater Cricket as played at Lords, because, though there must be rules which are adhered to, these rules in a house-party— especially where there are Women and Children—must be considerably modified if everybody is to enjoy the game. It is to be remembered that in games on which no Championship depend, it is far more important that they shall be good fun than that one side or t'other shall win—an automatic certainty, in any case. Nothing is more dull for a youthful or feminine member of the team than to be certain that it will be bowled first ball and spend the remainder of the day entirely by itself in a remote corner of the ground, waiting to field a ball that never comes. It is advocated, therefore, that

A. All bowlers should be given a chance in turn by the Captain, and Overs should consist of 9 balls instead of 6.

B. Good bowlers in bowling to the Small Fry should remember that Spofforth had his licence endorsed ; ' small ' bowling should be the rule in Small Cricket.

C. Good Batsmen will *never* remember that very long hits, continually repeated, are a nuisance, and can ruin the game ; before the game starts, therefore, Captains should consult and firmly fix certain boundaries, according to the nature of the ground. Such boundaries would penalise long hits ; a hit into the cornfield or the pig-stye might count 6 ; but it should, at the same time, be ' out.'

D. Where the players are few and small, first-bounce catches should be ' out.' L.B.W. should also be strictly enforced; this is essential, because our more womanly women still grossly exploit their skirts.

E. Where the players are small and few, and fielders scarce, both sides should field. Any players fielding against their own side should remember that it is far more necessary to field well than that their side should win.

F. A tennis-ball is the best sort of ball for this game. A cricket-stump is the best bat. But anything can be made to serve, as also for wickets.

G. Captains should be all-powerful, unless you have an Umpire; but an Umpire is no use unless you trust him."

SMALL HOCKEY

" Small Hockey is played as Ordinary Hockey; with a solid rubber ball if possible, and walking-sticks; but no freak sticks, cut specially for the purpose. Both sides of the stick may be used. Some ' bunting ' therefore will be unavoidable; but it should be reduced to a minimum.

" In Small Hockey there is no offside, and there is no circle. A goal may be shot anywhere beyond the half-way line. For ' Behind,' instead of a Bully, there is a free hit for the goal from the ' Go ' line; but after a goal is shot, there is always a new centre bully.

" Captains, as in Small Cricket, should be all-powerful, and should see strict enforcement of Stick Rule; sticks must *not* be raised above the shoulder, or the Hockey-Ground become a sacrificial altar to Brains and Beauty. Shoulder-height varies in all men, however; therefore, if our team happens to include Chaliapine or Little Tich, we must take our chances.

" Any number of players on a side; in proportioning his field afterwards, all the Captain has to remember is that there should be five times as many Forwards as there are Goal-Keepers."

TIERCE

" Or Twos-and-Threes. One player is 'He,' the others stand in a fairly wide circle in pairs, one in front of the other; but in one group there are three. The Behind Man in this group begins to run, and ' He ' has to try to catch him before or touch him before he slips into the circle and stands in front of any other pair. The moment he does so the Behind Man of that pair has to run and take his chance of being caught, as there must never be more than two people in a group. If 'He' touches his prey before it saves itself by joining a new group, 'He' instantly places himself in safety before one of the pairs, and the player just caught becomes 'He,' and chases the Third Man on the outside of the circle."

THE ROOF GAME

is played by two persons with a discarded tennis ball and a sloping roof. The ideal roof is 60 feet long, slopes at an angle of 110°, ends 8 feet from the ground and has a perfectly clear space in front of it   Each player in turn serves one ball from any position and at any speed. The ball must roll or bounce off the roof inside two imaginary walls projecting from the two ends of the roof at right angles to the front of the roof building. If the ball comes off the roof outside this imaginary space, it counts as a let, but the service passes. The receiver must catch the ball before it touches the ground. If he does so, neither scores ; if he fails, the server scores one point. In either event the service passes. The receiver scores one point if the server fails to reach the roof or throws the ball over the roof. In the latter event he must fetch it, as well as lose a point. A game is five points. All feints are legitimate, and there need be no delay between receiving and serving.

A chimney is a hazard : a ball may be served against it with such force as frequently to elude the receiver ; but if the server misses it he risks the penalties for throwing over the roof. This game can be played as a foursome.

If none of these games can be got through without trouble, there is always

TOM TIDDLER'S GROUND
or
TEAM-RACES

with or without obstacles. I have Spoken (*sitting down and kicking* J O H N). I call upon my dishonourable friend on the left to take the floor of the house.

L U C I A N : Yes, you unsociable animal !

JOHN (*mildly*) : As a matter of fact I have been noting down a few Problems for you.

ALICE (*plaintively*) : I'm not clever.

JOHN (*consulting his notes*) : My first lot is for persons with common sense. Shall I read ?

MOST OF US: Yes.

PROBLEM ONE

JOHN : " ' I will engage you,' said the Managing Director, ' at a salary of £100 per annum. You will have a half-yearly increase of £5—or, if you prefer it, a yearly increase of £20.' Which did the clerk choose, and why ? "

HAMBLETON (*after a feverish second*) : Why, it's obvious that twenty is more than twice five.

JOHN (*gently*): Work it out.

PROBLEM TWO

" Two vessels A and B hold milk and water respectively. A spoonful of milk is taken from A and introduced into B, where it is mixed up. A spoonful of the B mixture is then put into A. What is the proportion of the amount of water in A to the amount of milk in B ? "

PROBLEM THREE

A penniless tramp picks up a dollar in the United States. (The value of a U.S. dollar in the U.S. for the purposes of this problem is 5s.) He decides to have a drink, which costs him 2d. He puts down his dollar and gets in return a Mexican dollar. (The value of a Mexican dollar in the U.S. is 4s. 10d.) He then crosses the border into Mexico and decides to have a drink, which costs him 2d. He puts down his Mexican dollar of which the value in Mexico is 5s. and gets in return an American dollar. (The value of an American dollar in Mexico is 4s. 10d.) He then crosses the border into America and decides to have a drink which costs him 2d. He puts down . . . And so on *ad infinitum*. Who pays for his drinks ? "

LUCIAN : That reminds me—(*he sees an answering light in* ROBERT'S *eyes. They rise as one man and leave the room*).

PROBLEM FOUR

JOHN: " Two bowlers, A and B, have each taken 28 wickets for 60 runs. In the last match of the season A takes 1 wicket for 27 runs and B 4 wickets for 36 runs. Which bowler has now the better average? Why? "

GEORGE: *What?* Just let me take that down. (*He does.*)

JOHN: My next lot are Problems for the Intelligentsia.

ALICE (*slips away without a sound*).

PROBLEM FIVE

JOHN: " Classes are of two kinds; those which are members of themselves and those which are not. Instances of classes which are members of themselves are the class of non-humans, since the class of non-humans is itself non-human; and the class of classes, since the class of classes is itself a class. Instances of classes which are not members of themselves are the class of match boxes and the class of beetles, since in these cases the class of match boxes is not a match box and the class of beetles is not a beetle. Is the class of all classes which are not members of themselves, a member of itself or not a member of itself? " (*At this point the rest of the women stop fidgeting and go to bed.*)

PROBLEM SIX

JOHN: " Detect fallacies, if any, in the following:

(*a*) The unanswerable objection to an unanswerable objection is that it never *is* answered.

(*b*) It is most unlikely that the earth will ever be destroyed by colliding with a nebula or with another star or planet: it has never done so yet.

(*c*) Throughout any one day during the war the chances of a man being killed are five to two against. Throughout ten days, therefore, the chances of his being killed are fifty to twenty against. Hence the longer he stays out, the more do the chances of his not being killed exceed the chances of his being killed. Therefore the longer a man is at the front, the less likely he is to be killed."

FERDINAND: The relationship between the chances remains constant——

275

JOHN (*contemptuously*): Quite so! You mean, in short, that he is just as likely to be killed, no more and no less, if he stays out five minutes, as he is if he stays out five years. Very intelligent!

(GEORGE *resents the disturbance and retires with his cricket problem.*)

JOHN (*imperturbably*) : " Problem six (*d*)

$$4 - 10 = 9 - 15$$
$$\therefore 4 - 10 + \frac{25}{4} = 9 - 15 + \frac{25}{4}$$

Take square roots
$$\therefore 2 - \frac{5}{2} = 3 - \frac{5}{2}$$
$$\therefore 2 = 3$$

(*e*) In a certain village there is a barber; one barber only and no more. He is clean-shaven. The barber shaves all those and only those who do not shave themselves. Who shaves the barber?

(*f*) *The Short Proof of Determinism.* It is either true or false *now* that I shall be hanged to-morrow; therefore whether I shall be hanged to-morrow or not hanged to-morrow is already determined." (FERDINAND *utters a wordless noise—the Plain Man's protest—and removes himself.*)

JOHN : My next are Problems for the Intelligent:

PROBLEM SEVEN

" How would events upon the earth appear to a person observing them through a telescope stationed upon a planet moving away from the earth (a) with a velocity equal to that of light; (b) with a velocity greater than that of light? Should the answer to (b) suggest that the beginning of a man is a disturbance among worms, speculate upon the significance of this (i) for the law of cause and effect; (ii) for human dignity. (*Exit* HAMBLETON.)

PROBLEM EIGHT

JOHN: " If you go round the world travelling from west to east you gain a day, i.e. 24 hours. (Cp. Phineas Fogg in

"Round the World in Eighty Days.") What happens if, taking advantage of the facilities afforded by modern travel, you go round the world (a) in 24 hours; (b) in less than 24 hours? Should the answer to (b) suggest that you get back before you started; speculate upon the significance of this for the reality of time." (*He looks up to find himself alone. Methodically pockets his notes, consults his watch and murmurs philosophically*) : The realities of bed-time!

ON FOOD AND DRINK

"And cooks recorded frames of mind
In sad and subtle chops."

G. K. Chesterton.

ON FOOD AND DRINK

FOOD AND DRINK

Week-end cookery should be either very quick, a good meal produced in half an hour, or very slow, put on before you go off to tennis or to lazing.

However witty the talk, however shady the garden, however original the house and its furnishings, it won't be by these things alone that your week-ends will be judged for repetition, but also by the food you offer.

NOTABLE AND AMUSING FOOD

Serve unusual dishes that will be remembered and spoken of. Settle on a speciality and learn it up, be it the art of devilling, of making fritters, of serving *hors d'œuvres*, or of compounding a salad. Get an unusual, not a humdrum, cookery book and practice a few dishes between week-ends. Never let any dish be dull. Decorate the commoner foods into jolliness. Your guests eat with their eyes as well as with their palates and noses. Green cherries in grape fruit will be remembered (they can be bought in bottles). Boiled potatoes may be disguised by being mashed, made into balls, and rolled in grated cheese.

TINNED FOODS

Use tinned foods, but disguise them. No one should ever suspect that they are tinned. All tinned foods are improved by additions during the heating up. Never follow the directions on the tin for heating up : few saucepans are large enough to contain the unopened tin ; it takes longer than applying direct heat to the contents ; all but the most agile burn their fingers and spot their clothes when opening a heated tin.

Remember that Campbell's and Heinz's Tomato soups are not the only good soups on the market : there are chicken broths, asparagus. soups, clam chowders, pea soups.

S O U P S should have added to them a tablespoonful of marsala or other white wine, some red currant jelly, egg beaten in a cup of milk (always in tomato, spinach or celery). Use the water in which vegetables have been cooked to thin tinned soups. Serve with them some notable little addition, such as grated parmesan, puffed rice crisped in the oven, or fried cucumber cubes.

Tinned F I S H should be wrapped in buttered paper and heated in a covered frying-pan ; recooked in crumbs and cheese ; rebaked with a good lemon or anchovy sauce ; or poached in white wine or broth and served with shrimp, mixed gherkins, chipped olives, minced onion, anchovy paste, or a white sauce containing skinned grapes. (Skinned can be had in tins.)

To recook M E A T : place it on a bed of finely shredded vegetables, top with fried minced onion, pour gravy over, bring to the boil, then simmer, adding herbs, currant jelly, or a touch of vinegar. Some spiced sausages also renew the youth of a tinned stew to be served on a bed of rice or macaroni.

Of tinned V E G E T A B L E S : Baked beans may be baked again in a pie-dish lined and lidded with slices of bacon. Tinned sweet corn and succotash should be heated with additional butter, salt, pepper and sugar. Tinned peas should be drained, washed very thoroughly and treated like sweet corn, with the addition of a sprig of mint.

As for S W E E T S , the French fashion of fruit and cake may well replace elaborate creamed puddings or milk baked ones, wearisome even if coloured green or mixed with ginger or praliné. Fresh fruit alone, with some white wine and sugar, or with junket, is summer's ideal sweet. Failing that, have a plentiful stock of tinned fruits, to serve as they are or in jelly form.

To make J E L L I E S : Buy packets of jellies in preference to gelatin by the ounce, and follow the directions on the packets, telling you how to dissolve it in water in a mould. Buy plain in preference to flavoured jellies, so that you are not tied down to the taste of vanilla or lemon, adding your

282

own pet flavouring. For fruit jelly, add berries or cut-up fruit just as the mouldful begins to set. For a sponge jelly, whisk white of egg into the jelly just before it begins to set. For a milk jelly, pour on hot milk in place of water and stir in the mould over very hot water until it dissolves. Go on stirring over cold water until it begins to set.

Tinned cherries and tinned muscats are as nice and less hackneyed than peaches and pineapple. Don't buy the most expensive form of peaches : the cheaper kinds are packed riper. Don't buy pineapple chunks. Only sliced pineapple eliminates the wood-like core of the fruit. Hawaiian brands are the best.

In parenthesis : among untinned sweets, Z A M B A G - L I O N E is simple, memorable and delicious. For eight helpings, take six eegs, two glasses of marsala, Madeira, or any sweet wine, nine ounces of sugar, and one lemon. Put the yolks, sugar, lemon juice and wine into a thick saucepan. Whip the whites and add them to the rest. Thicken the mixture over an extremely slow heat, beating it furiously and continuously, and remembering that a Zambaglione boiled is a Zambaglione spoiled. When it is really thick, empty it into warmed glasses (to be eaten hot) or turn into a basin and go on beating it until it is cold. Teetotalers may make this dish with fruit juices.

W H E N B U Y I N G T I N N E D F O O D S avoid glass pre-serves. Rubber is not so durable a seal as solder. Ptomaine forms only when food is left in an open tin, or when the tin is imperfect (a puncture too small to be visible may be detected by rapping several tins with a pencil, when a defective one will ring flatter than others, as a false coin does).

HORS-D'ŒUVRE.

T O B E G I N A M E A L: *Hors-d'œuvres* should start a good dinner, unless there is *grape-fruit*. An alternative to grape-fruit is to serve an *orange* cut like the grape-fruit and, like it, moistened with maraschino and sugar.

As for the H O R S - D ' Œ U V R E S , don't limit yourself to sardines and tomato in oil. Try anchovy paste on cold egg slices ; tomato slices sprinkled with chopped onion and gherkin ; tomato anchovy and capers on hard-boiled eggs ; or just tomatoes stuffed with sardines or shrimp and chopped pickle. Cover the oddments with M A Y O N - N A I S E. It is simplest to buy a good brand, add a trifle of cream to it and pretend you made it yourself. But in that case remember not to serve it in the bottle. . .

Don't buy sardines in anything but olive oil. And buy your anchovies as anchovy strips, so as to be sure they are boned.

SHORT TIME COOKERY : THE GRIDIRON

Of all forms of cookery that allow you to get a meal ready after you come in and before your guests' appetites ruin their tempers, G R I D I R O N C O O K E R Y is the best. Cutlets, chops, steaks, even fish wrapped in greased paper, can be cooked between the wires before the fire. Steaks should first be placed very close to the heat to seal the juice, then moved to a cooler spot and cooked four minutes or so on each side, according to thickness. Salt only when on the dish. Kidneys are first-rate cooked like that, and then buttered and put on a skewer.

Food is given an unusual taste before grilling by being M A R I N A T E D , that is, steeped in a mixture of oil and vinegar to which herbs have been added. Steep for some hours.

Cooked between the wires or on a frying-pan, your steak or your fish will need a garnish as unusual as possible. Well-grilled steak dished with watercress and potatoes fried in deep fat is excellent—once. But next time try putting on top of your steak or fish a pat of S A V O U R Y B U T T E R . For this, work the butter with a spoon, season with pepper, and work in parsley chopped as finely as may be, or anchovy pulp ; pounded anchovy and sieved capers ; chopped shrimps ; pounded roes with a half-teaspoonful of vinegar to two ounces of butter ; or chopped watercress and gherkin.

As for S A U C E S , learn to make a perfect " Mother Sauce," and you can vary it as you like. To make a pint of white

284

mother sauce (the basis for all others), melt two ounces of butter in a pan over the gentlest possible heat ; work in an ounce of flour, cook very gently for five minutes, add a pint of milk and water and a saltspoonful of salt. Continue to stir and beat as it cooks. When creamy (in about five minutes' time) remove, and add another ounce of butter. This is the perfect white sauce. You can use pale broth or vegetable water if the milk is not available.

Any good flavour can be added—egg yoke (only do not let a sauce with egg yoke and butter boil) ; egg yoke and lemon juice (but add the juice after it is off the fire or the sauce will curdle) ; chopped capers ; white wine and tarragon ; nutmeg and onion ; mustard and lemon juice ; mussels ; mushrooms ; tomato purée ; grated parmesan ; mixed herbs and chablis ; pickles and chopped nuts.

SHORT TIME COOKERY : THE FRYING-PAN

Another form of quick cookery, for those who have neither a coal nor a gas fire suitable for grilling, is C H A F I N G - D I S H C O O K E R Y . This is done in a frying-pan with a cover to it, French fashion. The cover should be domed, so that the pan can be used, not only for frying, but to steam food. This is done by filling little pots, buttered inside and covered with buttered paper, and placing them in water in the covered pan. Fish, anchovy, cheese, or vegetable custards, minced meat and egg, the remains of any food in sauce, quails, made-up cutlets, olives or cucumber in rice and sauce—these are all things to be cooked in this way.

Apart from such poaching, foods are half fried, half steamed in a covered frying-pan with butter, seasoning and a little liquid. Uncovered it is used for plain frying, to scramble eggs, poach them, make omelettes and sweet pancakes.

The secret of making the best O M E L E T T E S is to with-draw the white of one egg for every six eggs used, and not to beat the eggs for too long. Omelettes containing mixed ham, potatoes, pimentoes, mushrooms, asparagus tips, and even fruit or jam, are easy to improvise. Pour the beaten eggs into a pan well covered with smoking lard, and then introduce the other materials. Fold one half of the omelette on the other, and gently slide the whole on to a hot plate.

Green salads may be made of many plants other than lettuce. Chicory, dandelion leaves, sorrel and white cabbage, for instance. They should be perfectly clean, perfectly dry and thickly coated with olive oil, before the dressing is added. The best D R E S S I N G for green salads is vinegar, oil, mustard, pepper, sugar and salt, in proportions varying according to taste, but always very thoroughly mixed.

Waldorf salad is made of equal parts of raw cooking apple and raw celery, sliced, disposed on a bed of lettuce, liberally garnished with half-walnuts, and dressed with a sweetened mayonnaise. Orange and lettuce ; shrimp and lettuce ; watercress and creamed cheese with nuts, are quite as easy to mix as lettuce and beetroot, and much more fun.

SANDWICH SUGGESTIONS

When you go picnicking you will, if a pastry hand, take little pies full of good mixtures, but the average provider of picnic fare trusts to sandwiches, good drinks, (hard and soft), hot coffee in thermos bottles, salted almonds, nuts, and perhaps raw steaks and bacon to be cooked over a camp fire on sticks. This is amusing because the food usually falls in and gets ruined. So be sure that the sandwiches are good.

Here are some fillings to be served, some in white bread, some in brown, some in rye bread, some in water biscuits and others in split scones : chopped hard-boiled egg and filleted anchovy ; cream cheese and jam (this in a scone) ; peanut butter and chopped olives ; peanut butter and raisins, or dates, or watercress ; Devonshire cream and honey ; " Gentleman's Relish " ; cold minced curry ; tomtao ketchup and fresh sliced tomato or lettuce ; chopped boiled beet and grated parmesan ; cream cheese, nuts and shredded pineapple ; cream cheese and olives ; currant jelly and chopped nuts ; chopped dates, cheese and nuts.

Don't butter sandwich bread, but if you like you may mix your filling with creamed butter and spread that. Pack your sandwiches as soon as cut in grease-proof paper.

BREAKFASTS

Don't worry about breakfast cooking. Bacon on toast or poached does well enough if you get unusual jams, or begin with fruit. Try orange and apple cut up, grated apple in glasses, or summer fruits with lemon juice. To fry crisp bacon, run the fat off and roll it as it cooks. Other breakfast dishes are : mashed potato balls with chopped sausage ; chopped egg and minced ham in white sauce on toast ; any hot sandwich ; scrambled egg and minced onion ; eggs cooked in butter (and cream, if that can be) in individual casseroles for five minutes. Season the butter and cream, break in the egg and bake, with a small spoonful of chopped chicken liver or minced ham or anchovy on top, if you will.

ADVICE TO THOSE WHO ATTEMPT TO SUPPLEMENT THEIR DIET FROM NATURE'S LARDER

FRESHWATER FISH: Trout and salmon should be eaten as soon as possible after being caught, as they are then at their best.

If the other freshwater fish you catch must be eaten, they should be soaked for at least 12 hours in brine. This removes both the slime and the taste of mud. Even carp or tench can in this way be made palatable.

MUSHROOMS AND TOADSTOOLS: Ordinary mushrooms are white on top, with a skin which peels readily, and have pinkish or black gills underneath, according to age. They grow in grass.

PUFFBALLS are round and white, puckered underneath. When young, they are excellent fried. They also grow in grass.

PARASOLLE mushrooms are white with brown flecks on top and with white gills. They are light and elegant in appearance, and grow in grass. Round the stem is a ring or band like the similar band frequently found on the shafts of umbrellas.

There is a BOLETUS TOADSTOOL found in woods which is excellent. It is dark brown on top, like a bun, and white and spongy underneath.

There is another boletus, yellow underneath, which it is also safe to eat.

ALL MUSHROOMS AND TOADSTOOLS are dangerous if they are not eaten fresh; therefore reject all botanist's specimens.

DON'T cook and attempt to eat YOUNG BRACKEN SHOOTS because the Japanese do. What suits the hardy races of the extreme East may not suit you.

DON'T cook YOUNG NETTLES as a substitute for spinach. It is a stringy one.

DON'T eat BOILED RHUBARB LEAVES. This practice caused a large number of deaths during the war.

DON'T take PLOVERS EGGS from a nest containing four. It is unkind to the parent birds, and at least two of the four will be addled.

DON'T cook things in clay.

N.B.—MICE IN HONEY should be imported from China, not prepared at home.

MENUS
QUICK

Clear soup with sausage rings.

Oiled, grilled herring served in buttered dish covered with butter melted with lemon juice, and cooked just a minute, then sprinkled chopped parsley and salt.

Coffee mousse; (whip cream till stiff; add little sugar and strong coffee made into syrup, with chopped nuts. Serve uncooked and cold).

QUICKISH

Escalopes of veal: season the veal pieces slightly, brown in butter on quick fire, cover pan and simmer ten minutes. Add half a cup gravy with lemon juice, cooking until gravy is reduced, only just covering the veal.

Lettuce, nut and olive salad.

Deep-fat-fried potato fingers.

Milk jelly with ginger in it.

VERY QUICK

Slices of cold mutton steeped in olive oil, vinegar and herbs, dipped in breadcrumbs and fried. Served with mint, red currant and orange rind jelly.

Cheesed potato balls and lettuce salad.
Stewed prunes in claret (boil steeped prunes in syrup, adding claret ten minutes before removing from fire).

HALF-HOUR
Grape-fruit with green cherries.
Leg of lamb cut into steaks, sprinkled chopped onion, wrapped in cabbage leaves (or bacon), buttered, floured, browned and cooked half an hour in casserole, with little hot water.
Fruit in white wine with cream into which chopped nuts are beaten.

HALF-HOUR AGAIN
Grilled cutlets ; mint jelly on orange rounds.
Tiny mashed potato balls, with bit of olive in centre ; green peas.
Port wine jelly and cream (made beforehand).

FOR A BEGINNER
Tinned spinach soup with egg beaten in.
Rognons en brochettes (kidneys, bacon and sausages grilled on a skewer).
Straw potatoes, deep fat fried.
Cake-covered fruit and cream.

FOR A SUMMER EVENING
Clear soup with tiny diamonds of cheesed toast.
Hake or haddock grilled with capers.
Orange and lettuce salad with mayonnaise.
Strawberries, and cream or claret.

AMBITIOUS
Hors-d'œuvres.
Casserole of duck with orange slices and rind ; lettuce, shredded celery or beetroot.
Pancakes in fruit syrup.

ONE SLOW-COOKING DISH
Orange maraschino cups.
Stuffed steak with tomato, onion and beet ; pineapple, lettuce and tomato salad.
Fruit salad.

DRINK

For hard drinkers, whisky, gin and the vermouths, for soft drinkers, tea, coffee and ginger-beer are the commonest products of the English country pub. But imagination and bold experiment can break this monotony with many happy improvisations.

" Ginandit " is the weary walker's counsel of despair. Any enterprising week-end pub, or cottage, will possess ingredients from which one or other of the following may be compounded :

COCKTAILS

EAST INDIAN : Equal parts of French vermouth and sherry, with a dash of orange bitters.

WEST INDIAN : Two parts rum (preferably Bacardi's) to one part fresh lime or lemon juice, with some sugar dissolved in it, or failing this, " Kia-ora."

HAWAIIAN : Four parts gin, two parts orange juice and one part curacoa (or any other of the orange liqueurs).

SIDE-CAR : Equal parts of fresh lemon juice (no alternative), cointreau (or one of the orange liqueurs) and brandy.

SATAN'S WHISKER (*straight*) : Of Italian Vermouth, French Vermouth, gin and orange juice, two parts each ; of Grand Marnier one part ; orange bitters.

Ditto (*curled*) : For the Grand Marnier substitute an equal quantity of orange curacao.

JOHN WOOD : Italian Vermouth, four parts ; Irish whiskey and lemon juice, two parts each ; Kummel, one part ; angostura bitters.

MR. SUTTON'S GIN-BLIND (*to be drunk with discretion*) : Six parts gin, three parts curacao, two parts brandy and a dash of orange bitters.

NOTE ON THE USE OF BITTERS : When cocktails are mixed in bulk, any bitters should be introduced in the proportion of one half to one teaspoonful per pint. In more intimate drinking, delicacy of flavour and economy of material are secured by rinsing each glass with bitters, which are then returned to the bottle, while the glass is filled with a mixture from which bitters have been omitted.

If possible, ALL COCKTAILS should stand on ice for at least half an hour before shaking and taking. If you cannot wait so long, you must adulterate your mixture with ice. A large jug, and an egg-whisk (or even a fork) efficiently replace the shaker. The glasses should be as cold as possible before the cocktail is poured out.

ICED DRINKS

GINGER-BEER: (*a*) with gin and lemon or lime juice, preferably fresh, but, if need be, " Kia-ora " or Southwells ; (*b*) (for sweet-tooths) with cointreau and orange juice.
(There is no bottled substitute for orange juice, whatever you may have seen in the shops.)
Strong, cold, black COFFEE with a wineglassful of brandy to a quart and some ice.
For people who can bear to be seen drinking it: Equal parts of GIN and CRÈME DE MENTHE, with plenty of cracked ice.
JOHN COLLINS: The juice of two oranges and one lemon with an equal measure of gin, some soda water and ice.
BAVARIAN CUP: Mix a small wineglassful of cherry brandy (or plain brandy) with a bottle of white wine, and add crushed strawberries and ice *ad lib.*
CIDER CUP: Three large bottles of sparkling cider, a pint of old Marsala, a little sugar, a lot of lemon rind, two bottles of soda water and maraschino or brandy quant : suff :
RAJAH'S PEG : A claret glass of old brandy in a pint of dry champagne.
MINT JULEP: Pack a tumbler as tightly as possible with alternate layers of finely cracked ice and sprigs of mint, freshly picked and bruised ; fill the interstices with whisky (rye if available, otherwise Irish or, if need be, Scotch). This tastes as good as it smells. It is drunk by degrees, as it melts, and through a straw.
CASSIS (black-currant syrup made in France) is obtainable in Soho, and, when mixed with soda-water and ice, makes a delicious " soft " drink.

COLD TEA should be made as follows: Steep the leaves in *cold water* (the same proportion as you use when boiling) for 12 hours and then strain.

HOT DRINKS

TEA with rum, lemon juice and a shaving of lemon peel.

MULLED CLARET (1) *For Boys :* Warm (but do not boil) the wine with nutmeg, cinnamon, cloves, sugar and lemon rind. (2) *For Men :* Ditto, adding dry port one part to six of claret. (3) *For Heroes :* As for boys, adding one part port to three parts claret and as much old brandy as you think the company can stand.

RUM PUNCH: one part rum, one part whisky and two parts (or a trifle less) water, heated with sugar, cinnamon, nutmeg, cloves and dried orange and lemon peel.

HANDY PUNCH: to two bottles of whisky and one of rum, add an equal quantity of water. Heat these with a little nutmeg and cinnamon, the juice of two lemons and sugar to taste. When it is very hot, set it alight with a red-hot poker and, after a moment's admiration, blow out the flames.

RED CURRANT TEA is a good hot " soft " drink. It is made by pouring boiling water on plenty of red currant jelly and adding a squeeze of lemon juice. Black currant jam will make BLACK CURRANT TEA.

> " 'Tis his great happiness that he is distempered, thereby to have an opportunity of experiencing the efficacy and sweetness of the remedies which you have so judiciously propounded. I approve 'em all."
>
> Congreve, *Squire Trelooby*.

FIRST AID IN DIVERS CRISES
MEDICAL, SURGICAL & GASTRONOMICAL

*N.B. that the drugs herein recommended may be supplied by
a Chemist without a physician's prescription.*

Now we give you Physic and other Remedies for certain
Accidents, Sicknesses and Infirmities which may trouble
your week-ends. But should any of the graver mishaps
befall you of which we treat hereafter, remember that
our advices must be used only to allay the harm and to
beguile the time while your Physician is delayed. Remember also that the drugs are occasional drugs, to be
used rarely and compounded with discretion. For, though
our simples be culled from venerable masters and our
compounds be furnished worthily and though your apothe-
cary be scrupulous to the last minim, yet these alone shall
not avail to save you.

AGAINST STINGS AND BITES

If Stung by a Bee or Wasp, extract first the sting by pressing
on to the puncture with a small key. Now neutralise the
Venom by washing the wound with a solution of Ammonia
or Potash.

Good against the Sting of all Insects, including Midges and
Mosquitoes, is the application, with a pencil of camel's hair,
of an analgesic blended of Acid Carbolic gr.v, Tr. Iodidi
mx, Potass. Iodidi gr.xx and Aqua dest. ad ℥i. To
anticipate an assault apply to vulnerable areas an epithem
of Ol. Eucalypti ℨiss, Sp. Camphoræ ℥i and Lin. Saponis
ad ℥ii; or use as a cosmetic Carmine gr.i, Ol. Eucalypti
m xv and Pulv. Cret. Gall. ℥ii. Man does not succumb
so readily to these as the Harvester, the Midge and the
Mosquito.

To take away the Stinging of Nettles use the above application; but, where there is Dock nearby, apply of this a
bruised leaf to the area of stinging and chant the following
Cantrap:

> Out Nettle, in Dock:
> Dock shall have a new smock.

L *

To search for Harvesters, dig in the skin with a needle first heated in a candle flame ; and afterwards cleanse the spot with iodine.

To search for Fleas, be seated on a white and woolly blanket, for this most readily entangles and makes visible your enemy. But some hold that to clap an open bottle of chloroform or a wet cake of soap upon the spot attacked is better.

HARM BY VENOMOUS SNAKES

Against the Harm by Venomous Snakes take measures to prevent the poison from diffusing itself through the system generally and to destroy what is already in the wound. To achieve the former object a tourniquet may be improvised by tying a handkerchief loosely round the limb between the wound and the heart, placing a short stick in the ring bandage thus formed and twisting this until the limb is tightly compressed. Now withdraw the venom locally by sucking the wound. (This proceeding is dangerous only in that it creates a reputation for courage and presence of mind which is difficult to maintain, except in the rare advent of another case of snake bite. It is, however, quite unnecessary to swallow the venom and one may go far to undo the unfortunate impression of heroism by using an antiseptic mouth wash at the earliest possible moment.) It is good to encourage bleeding by bathing the fang apertures with warm water and to extend the wounds down to the subcutaneous tissues with a clean, sharp knife. If the means be available, apply crystals of potassium permanganate or a strong Carbolic acid solution to the wound. Give also, to counteract the severe shock, good doses of whisky or brandy, repeated several times if necessary. Some people prefer sal volatile in doses of a teaspoonful to a wineglass of water. No one knows the reason for this.

BURNINGS AND SCALDINGS

Burnings and Scaldings by Fire and Water and Corrosive Substances may, when slight, be treated by pouring over them ordinary Salad Oil, or a mixture of Olive (or Linseed) Oil and Lime Water in equal parts, and then covering with a dressing of lint soaked in oil. Remember that it is necessary to exclude air from the burn as quickly as possible, to administer stimulants, and on no account to break a blister. Severe burns must not be touched by the untutored hand.

BLISTERS

The popular Indulgence of Biting off Blood Blisters is strongly to be deprecated. The proper treatment is to sterilise the skin that covers them with an antiseptic and then to evacuate the blood with a needle which has previously been reddened in a flame.

TO STAUNCH BLOOD

To Staunch Blood that oozes gently or that flows in a continuous stream of dark purple, it is sufficient to apply a pad of lint on which Iodine has been poured and then to fix this by means of a handkerchief, scarf or bandage.

But when the blood is scarlet and issues from the limb in a series of jets, you must act with coolness and promptitude. Press the thumb or forefinger tightly to the wound, while another improvises a tourniquet, which must be bound to the thigh or upper arm between the bleeding point and the heart. The only modification of the already described tourniquet (vide *Venomous Snakes*) is that now there is included within the folds of the handkerchief a smooth pebble which presses directly upon the artery when the tourniquet has been fixed in position. When the bleeding has been arrested it is good to cleanse the wound and apply a simple Iodine dressing. Unless collapse has occurred it is forbidden to administer stimulants until the Surgeon has taken measures to prevent recurrence of bleeding.

EPISTAXIS (NOSE-BLEED)

When the Nose bleeds do not bow the head over a basin, or you will very soon need another. Sit with the head slightly thrown back and apply Cold Water Compresses to the root of the nose, the face and between the shoulder blades. It is good in moderately severe cases to inhale the Vapour of Turpentine or a Snuff of powdered Alum. Where these methods fail or are not available, it is an emergency measure to plug into the nostrils long, narrow strips of gauze, packing these as far back as possible and continuing until the whole nasal cavity is filled.

EMERGENCY ANTISEPTICS

The following Emergency Antiseptics may be used in any case where sterilisation and antisepsis are indicated :

Methylated Spirits with an equal bulk of water ;

Whisky similarly tampered with ;

Salt, a dessertspoonful dissolved in a tumbler of warm water ;

Vinegar.

Tincture of Iodine should, however, be preferred to any of these.

SYNCOPE

When Syncope (fainting) is imminent, let the sufferer clasp his head between his knees and the crisis may pass. Should unconsciousness supervene, keep the head low, loosen the clothing and hold to the nose smelling salts or burnt feathers. It is pleasant and fitting that the patient celebrate the first moment when he is able to stand upright by partaking of a fluid ounce of brandy or whisky. Sal Volatile should not be withheld on grounds of principle.

PERIPALPEBRAL ECCHYMOSIS

Peripalpebral Ecchymosis (black eye). First counteract the swelling and discoloration of this and every other manner of bruise by gently rubbing in the tincture of Arnica Flowers or a solution of Witch Hazel Leaves (Liquor Hamamelidis). Then apply with a moderately tight bandage a compress made of cotton wool or lint steeped in cold water. *When bruised all over* and feeling shaken but not faint there is much relief in a hot bath. This may be followed by the use of an embrocation made from Spr. Vini Rectif. and Liq. Ammon. Acet. of each ℥iss and Aqua Camphoræ ℥viii, which is gently applied to the skin and allowed to evaporate.

TO SOOTHE THE FACE

To soothe the Face tormented by the Sun and Wind, use an anodyne compounded of Acid Hydrochlor. mxv, Acid

300

Citric ʒi, Ess. Rosæ alb. mxxx, Glycerin and Sp. rectificat. of each ʒiv and Aqua dest. ad ʒiv.

To withstand the Pigmentation of Freckles, wash in Sour Milk or in Buttermilk; or from the Apothecary obtain their active principle in the following formula : Acid Lactic (10 per cent) ʒii, Glycerini ʒss, Ess. Rosæ Alb. ʒiss, Tr. Benzoin ʒi and Aqua ad ʒi. This should be dabbed on the face with cotton wool twice each day.

AFTER EXPOSURE

After Exposure to Wind and Rain it is good to seek the *Abortion of Nasal Catarrh.* Take, therefore, immediately on returning home, of Calomel Gr.iii and a hot bath. At night, another hot bath should be followed by Pulv. Ipecac. Co.gr.xv, taken in a warmed bed. Take now, for not more than three days, a pill compounded of Quinine Sulphate and Powdered Camphor, of each gr.ss and fluid Extract of Belladonna Root m ⅛, four times a day. These things are inimical to the thin rheum.

TO REMEDY THE TOOTHACHE

Where there is no Doctor or Dentist, but only an Apothe-cary, *remedy the Toothache and the Gumboil* by applying cotton wool saturated in Tr.Opii, Chloroform, Sp. Camph., and Tr. Pyrethri, of each ʒi, which is a potent analgesic. But if there be a Dentist or a Doctor, shun this like poison (which it is) and go at once to the one or the other; for only in them is Salvation.

GOOD AGAINST THE MEGRIMS

Good against the Megrims, Neuralgias and all manners of Aches and Pains is a cachet made of Phenacetin gr.v, Aspirin gr.v and Caffein Citrate gr.iii

SEA–SICKNESS

On Becoming Indifferent to the Fate of your Ship, pack the ears firmly with gauze until the pressure on the tympanic membrane can be felt. It is useful to take of Chloretone gr.v in a cachet, repeating two-hourly if necessary three or four times. If Chloretone disagrees, compromise with the semicircular canals by taking of Syr. Chloral ʒii, Pot. Bromid. gr. xxx, and Aqua Chlorof. ad ʒiss, one teaspoonful every five minutes till relief or sleep occurs. It is best to lie on the right side with the knees drawn up to the abdomen.

SUNSTROKE

Upon such as are Overcome by the Sun, cold water should be dashed, especially over the head, neck and chest   Apply frequently to the forehead cloths wrung out of iced water ; and ice itself is very good.

SPRAINS

Before treating a Sprain of the Ankle or any other Joint remember that there may be a graver injury present ; a dislocation or even fracture of one of the component bones of the joint. But as emergency measures (having transported the victim home, with the limb in the position that gives greatest ease) remove the clothing, put the patient on a couch and, under the guidance of his sensations, rest the limb on cushions, preferably in such a way that it is well elevated. Now try the application of cold compresses ; or, if these fail to relieve pain, of hot fomentations, which should be tightly bandaged over the joint. It is good, if pain is excessive, to apply a teaspoonful of laudanum to the fomentation.

Treat Tennis Elbow and Jumper's Sprain by massaging the injured part and applying a firm bandage. Bathing alternately with hot and cold water is soothing and beneficial.

TO STAY THE HICQUET

To stay the Hicquet drink water backwards. This art consists in applying the lips to the far side of the glass and bending forward the head and body till drinking becomes possible. As a prophylactic measure it should be practised secretly.

Another method is to sip slowly a glass of water with both ears and nostrils stopped. A few drops of essence of peppermint on sugar are very effective in the case of such patients as cannot take water.

FIRST AID IN DIVERS CRISES

RELIEF OF THE WINDY SPASMS

For the Immediate Relief of the Windy Spasms take on sugar Oil of Cajuput, five minims; or of Sp. Ætheris Composita thirty minims, repeated every fifteen minutes if necessary

POISONED FOOD

After Partaking of Poisoned Food it is correct to send for a doctor. (It is good to inform him of the purpose for which he is needed.) Meanwhile provoke vomition by titillating the back of the throat with a finger or by administering, every five minutes until successful, any of the following emetics :
Salt : a tablespoonful to a tumbler of water.
Mustard : a teaspoonful to a tumbler of water ; or Ipecacuanha wine, a teaspoonful.
Meanwhile the patient should be put to bed, hot bottles and hot foments applied to the Abdomen and, if there are signs of collapse, brandy or other stimulants administered. Finally give an ounce of castor oil. These measures are good against Surfeits of Wholesome Meats and Drinks as well as other forms of food poisoning.

BEFORE HOBNAILING THE LIVER

Before Occasions devoted to Hobnailing the Liver it is recommended to take a half to one ounce of Olive Oil. The Parkinson Herbal states that " if one doe eate five or sixe bitter Almonds before he fall into drinking company, it will keepe him from being overtaken more than the rest." On the occasion itself, deal with *Imminent Emergencies* by partaking of the following sedative : Acid Hydrocyan Dil. miv, Tr. Nuc. Vom. mx, Tr. Aurant, mx, Aqua Cinn. ad ℥i. But to such as cannot themselves partake administer a potion of Liq. Ammon. Acet. ℥i and await the future with kindly interest.

THE MORNING AFTER

On the Morning After, comfort the cold and feeble brain by recalling the warning of Mayster Isaac Judæus who saith : " It is unpossyble for them that drinketh overmoche water in theyr youth to come to ye æge that God ordained them."

If it matters little to you whether the age that God ordained be reached or no, drink the following cordial : Take of Sp.Ammon.Aromat. mx, Sodii Bic. gr. xv, Tr. Capsici miii, Tr. Card. Co. ʒi, Tr. Zingib. Fort.mv, Tr.Cinc. Co.mx, Tr.Nuc.Vom.mx, Sp.Chlorof.mx and Water of Orange Flowers up to ʒi. Take also of Caffein Cit. gr.v, Acid Cit. gr.x, Tr. Aurant mv, and Water up to ʒi. And adding two tablespoonfuls of the first to two of the second drink whilst the effervescence lasts.

Some recommend—if only the head suffers—to take of Calcium Lactate, Gr. xxx.

WHEN COCKTAILS FAIL

If one be overcome by such *mishap or weariness* that even cocktails fail to cure his apathy, let him try this elixir : Ext. Turneræ liq. (B.P.C.) and Syr. Glycerophosph. Co., of each ʒi, and Decoctum Hordei ad ʒi, and he may still rise to the occasion.

Such are the ills that commonly befall those who walk abroad with their fellows to enjoy the pleasures of the country.

Should you ail anything else then " all the Nation are already Physitians, . . . every one you meet, whether man or woman will prescribe you a medecine for it."

But take their medicine, like ours, with circumspection, Reader.

LIST OF GREAT POEMS

CONTAINED IN MANY MEMORIES AND MOST
ANTHOLOGIES AND THEREFORE OMITTED
FROM THIS BOOK

Psalm 23 . . . The " Great Bible " version.
  " The Lord is my Shepherd "

O Mistress Mine . . . . W. Shakespeare.
  " O mistress mine, where are you
                roaming ? "

Fear no more . . . . . W. Shakespeare.
  " Fear no more the heat of the sun "
  (And the Sonnets and many more lyrics by
                the same author.)

Sweet content . . . . . T. Dekker.
  "Art thou poor, yet hast thou golden
                slumbers "

Delight in Disorder . . . R. Herrick.
  "A sweet disorder in the dress "

To the virgins to make much of time . R. Herrick.
  " Gather ye rosebuds while ye may "

Lycidas . . . . . J. Milton.
  " Yet once more, O ye laurels, and once
                more "

Upon Westminster Bridge . . W. Wordsworth.
  " Earth has not anything to show
                more fair "

Evening on Calais Beach . . . W. Wordsworth.
  " It is a beauteous evening, calm
                and free "

The World . . . . . W. Wordsworth.
  " The world is too much with us ;
                late and soon "

LIST OF GREAT POEMS NOT IN THIS BOOK

Ode to the West Wind . . . P. B. Shelley.
"O wild west wind, thou breath of
Autumn's being"

Ode on a Grecian Urn . . . . J. Keats.
"Thou still unravished bride of
quietness"

To Autumn . . . . . . J. Keats.
"Season of mists and mellow
fruitfulness"

Ode to a Nightingale . . . . J. Keats.
"My heart aches and a drowsy numb-
ness pains"

Sonnets from the Portuguese, III . E. B. Browning.
"Go from me. Yet I feel that I
shall stand"

Sonnets from the Portuguese, V . E. B. Browning.
"When our two souls stand up erect
and strong"

To Helen . . . . . . E. A. Poe.
"Helen, thy beauty is to me"

Omar Khayyám . . . . E. Fitzgerald.
(Selections according to taste)

Home thoughts from abroad . . R. Browning.
"O to be in England"

Last Lines . . . . . . E. Brontë.
"No coward soul is mine"

Departure . . . . . . C. Patmore.
"It was not like your great and
gracious ways"

A Farewell . . . . . . C. Patmore.
"With all my will, but much against
my heart"

Love in the Valley . . . . G. Meredith.
"Under yonder beech tree, single on the
greensward"

LIST OF GREAT POEMS NOT IN THIS BOOK

The South-wester . . . . G. Meredith.
  " Day of the cloud in fleets, O day "

A Birthday . . . . . C. G. Rossetti.
  " My heart is like a singing bird "

Remember . . . . . C. G. Rossetti.
  " Remember me when I am gone away "

Romance . . . . . R. L. Stevenson.
  " I will make you brooches and toys for
          your delight "

The Hound of Heaven . . . F. Thompson.
  " I fled him down the nights and down
          the days "

The lake Isle of Innisfree . . . . W. B. Yeats.
  " I will arise and go now, and go to
          Innisfree "

When you are old . . . . . W. B. Yeats.
  " When you are old and grey and full
          of sleep "

For the Fallen . . . . . L. Binyon.
  " With proud thanksgiving, the mother
          of her children "

The Song of Honour . . . . R. Hodgson.
  " I climbed a hill as light fell short "

An Epitaph . . . . . W. de la Mare.
  " Here lies a most beautiful lady "

The Shropshire Lad   (In general) . A. E. Housman.*

* Mr. Housman does not allow his poems to appear
          in anthologies.

ACKNOWLEDGEMENT

T H E editors have to thank all living poets whose work is to be found in this book for permission to include their poems. They are similarly indebted to the literary executors of Rupert Brooke, Samuel Butler, James Elroy Flecker, George Meredith, Alice Meynell, Walter Raleigh, Robert Louis Stevenson and Francis Thompson.

They further acknowledge with thanks permission from the following publishers to reprint poems appearing in the books here enumerated : Messrs. G. Bell & Sons : The Unknown Eros, by Coventry Patmore. Messrs. Burns & Oates : Poems, by Mr. G. K. Chesterton ; Collected Poems of Alice Meynell ; Collected Works of Francis Thompson ; The Flower of Peace, by Mrs. Tynan Hinkson ; Poems, by J. B. Tabb. Messrs. Jonathan Cape : Collected Poems of Mr. W. H. Davies ; Samuel Butler's Notebooks. Messrs. Chatto & Windus : Leda, by Mr. Aldous Huxley ; Argonaut and Juggernaut, by Mr. Osbert Sitwell ; Poems, by R. L. Stevenson. Messrs. Constable : Collected Works of George Meredith ; Poems by W. Raleigh. Messrs. Dent : The Wild Knight, by Mr. G. K. Chesterton. Messrs. Duckworth : Sonnets and Verse, by Mr. Hilaire Belloc. Messrs. Heinemann : Selected Poems, by Mr. Robert Frost ; War Poems, by Mr. Siegfried Sassoon. Messrs Hodder & Stoughton : Poems, by Mr. J. C. Squire. Messrs. Longmans, Green & Co. : Child's Garden of Verses, by R. L. Stevenson. Messrs. Macmillan : Collected Poems of T. E. Brown ; Late Lyrics, by Mr. Thomas Hardy ; Poems, by Mr. Ralph Hodgson ; Songs of England, by Alfred Austin ; Songs from the Clay, by Mr. James Stephens ; The Hill of Vision, by Mr. James Stephens ; Later Poems, by Mr. W. B. Yeats. Messrs. Methuen : Wine and Water, by Mr. G. K. Chesterton ; Collected Poems, by Mr. W. H. Davies. Messrs. Grant Richards : Little Poems, by Walter Leaf. The Poetry Bookshop : Spring Morning, by Mrs. Frances Cornford ; Autumn Midnight, by Mrs. Frances Cornford ; Strange Meetings, by Mr. Harold

ACKNOWLEDGEMENT

Monro; The "Georgian Poetry" anthologies. Messrs.
Elkin Mathews and Mr. Martin Secker: Collected Poems
of J. E. Flecker. Mr. Martin Secker: Pier Glass, by Mr.
Robert Graves; Verses, by Miss Viola Meynell. Messrs
Sidgwick & Jackson: Collected Poems of Rupert Brooke;
The Dark Fire, by Mr. Walter Turner.

They are also obliged to the following music collectors,
editors and publishers for permission to include the songs
here enumerated: Miss Lucy Broadwood: "The trees
they do grow high." Sir Richard Terry and Messrs. J.
Curwen & Sons: "Billy Boy" and "Shenandoah," from
The Shanty Book. Miss Kaipeles (executor of Cecil
Sharp) and Messrs. Novello for "A-roving." Messrs.
J. Curwen & Sons: "The Wraggle Taggle Gipsies."
Mr. Herbert Hughes: "The Shan Wan Wocht" and
"The old man that lived near hell." The Rev. Maunsell
Bacon: "The Mallard." Mr. E. J. Moeran: "Mrs.
Dyer." Messrs. Erskine Macdonald: "The Last Long
Mile" and "And when I die," both from More Tommy's
Tunes. Mr. G. H. Marston: "The Fire Ship." Messrs.
Schirmer of New York: "Chicka hanka." Messrs. James
Brown & Son of Glasgow: "Can't you dance the polka?"
from Sea Songs and Shanties. Messrs. Schott: "Mar-
ishka," from Hungarian Melodies. Messrs. Lengnick:
"The Easter Hymn" from Deutsche Geistliche Lieder;
and further, to Miss Jane Joseph for her translation of
"Ideo gloria in excelsis"; to the Editors of the English
Hymnal for their arrangement of Bunyan's hymn; to
Messrs. James Brown for the words of "The Rio
Grande"; and to Baron Beaverbrook for "The Jones
Boys."

INDEX OF POEMS
(FIRST LINES)

INDEX OF POEMS

INDEX OF POEMS

315

INDEX OF POEMS

INDEX OF SONGS

317

Look, what thy memory cannot contain
Commit to these waste blanks, and thou shalt find
Those children nurs'd, deliver'd from thy brain,
To take a new acquaintance of thy mind.
These offices, so oft as thou wilt look,
Shall profit thee, and much enrich thy book.

Shakespeare.

+B:Praised be the Lord
        A: Praised be the Lord
                T: Praised

be the Lord
+For his hand hath wrought a

mighty and marvellous thing A&T

Praised be the Lord, the Lord

be praised on earth T&B: And

by his mercy hath trodden our

foes underfoot A&T: Sing to

his praise in the sky (A ll:

And called him wonderful,

merciful, great and holy ruler

of the world.

POEMS

325

POEMS

SONGS

341